Recommended
SHORT BREAK HOLIDAYS
IN BRITAIN
1991

Short Break Holidays
throughout Britain
in Recommended, Registered or
otherwise Approved Establishments

*Fully described and illustrated
for direct booking*
WITH MAPS

FHG PUBLICATIONS

Other FHG Publications

Recommended Country Hotels of Britain
Recommended Wayside Inns of Britain
Pets Welcome!
Bed and Breakfast in Britain
The Golf Guide: Where to Play/Where to Stay
London's Best Bed and Breakfast Hotels

ISBN 1 85055 131 6
© FHG Publications Ltd. 1991
Cover photographs: Ivan J. Belcher
Cover design: Sheila Begbie
No part of this publication may be reproduced by any means or transmitted without the permission of the Publishers.

For pictures on pages 132 and 133, thanks to Edinburgh Marketing.

Cartography by David L. Fryer & Co., Henley-on-Thames
Maps are based on Ordnance Survey maps with the permission of Her Majesty's Stationery Office, crown copyright reserved.

Typeset by RD Composition Ltd., Glasgow.
Printed and bound in Great Britain by Richard Clay & Co., Bungay, Suffolk.

Distribution. **Book Trade:** Moorland Publishing, Moor Farm Road, Ashbourne, Derbyshire DE6 1HD (Tel: 0335 44486. Fax: 0335 46397). **News Trade:** UMD, 1 Benwell Road, Holloway, London N7 7AX (Tel: 071-700 4600. Fax: 071-607 3352).

Published by FHG Publications Ltd., Abbey Mill Business Centre, Seedhill, Paisley PA1 1JN (Tel: 041-887 0428 Fax: 041-889 7204).

Recommended
SHORT BREAK HOLIDAYS IN BRITAIN

PUBLISHER'S INTRODUCTION

OUR ENTRIES Only hotels and other holiday proprietors with an accepted recommendation, approval or rating are included. We do not inspect or recommend individual advertisers as such, but all entries have agreed to the principle of inspection by the Publishers if this should be necessary.

As you look through RECOMMENDED SHORT BREAK HOLIDAYS you will see other features which we hope will help in your holiday choice. All entries are illustrated, each has a description of the property, its amenities and facilities and points of special interest. 'Short Break' terms are presented in as standardised a way as possible. Please note that prices etc. are correct as we go to press but should be confirmed, along with any other details that are important to you.

SYMBOLS We use a small group of symbols to indicate features of common interest. Are pets accepted; are there reduced prices for children; are there facilities for the disabled; are there special Christmas breaks? The symbols are arranged in the same order so that looking down each page will give a quick comparison.

Crown ratings are given where appropriate. Please note that lack of Crowns may simply mean that the advertiser has still to be inspected (the waiting list is long) and it can also mean that there are special factors which make Crown rating inappropriate.

The [TA] symbol means that you can ask a Travel Agent to make your bookings and he can be sure that he will receive a commission for his efforts — Travel Agents cannot work for nothing!

ENQUIRIES AND BOOKINGS It is very easy to book yourself using the full address and/or telephone details given for each entry. Give full details of dates (with an alternative), numbers and any special requirements. Ask about any points in the holiday description which are not clear and make sure that prices and conditions are clearly explained. You should receive confirmation in writing and a receipt for any deposit or advance payment. If you book well in advance, confirm your arrival details nearer the time.

CANCELLATIONS A holiday booking is a form of contract with obligations on both sides. If you have to cancel, give as much notice as possible. The longer the notice the better the chance that your host can replace your booking and therefore refund any payments. If the proprietor cancels in such a way that causes serious inconvenience, he may have obligations to you which have not been properly honoured. Take advice if necessary from such organisations as the Citizen's Advice Bureau, Consumer's Association, Trading Standards Office, Local Tourist Office, etc., or your own solicitor.

COMPLAINTS It's best if any problems can be sorted out at the start of your holiday. You should therefore try to raise any complaints on the spot. If you do not, or if the problem is not solved, you can contact the organisations mentioned above. You can also write to us. We will follow up the complaint with the advertiser — but we cannot act as intermediaries or accept responsibility for holiday arrangements.

Peter Clark, Publishing Director

Odell Village, Bedfordshire.

John Carter introduces . . .

John Carter has been a travel journalist for over 25 years. First as Travel Editor of the Kemsley (later Thomson) group of newspapers, then Travel Correspondent of The Times *and now Travel Editor of* Good Housekeeping *magazine.*

He is the author of a best selling paperback 100 Great British Weekends *(Pan Books, 1983) and of* Chandler's Travels *(Quiller Press, 1985), a biography of one of the travel trade's more colourful characters, Harry Chandler.*

However, John Carter is probably best known as a television reporter and presenter. For many years he co-presented the BBC TV Holiday *programmes which he originally helped to create, before moving to the popular ITV series* Wish You Were Here.

A few of us were recently discussing holiday trends, and came to the not unexpected conclusion that the majority of people are content to find a beach and some sunshine and take it easy for a couple of weeks. We agreed that a growing number were choosing a "do it yourself" option but that the "Sun and Sand" package remained a winner.

Then the conversation turned to other forms of holidaymaking and to the growing trend for second holidays, taken usually in spring or autumn. Somebody mentioned the "educational factor" of such short breaks – a conversation-stopper if ever I heard one! It certainly stopped that conversation, for the idea of a holiday in a classroom, brushing up on your differential calculus, was something none of us could endure.

Afterwards, I realised that "educational factor" is another of the holiday trade's unfortunate terms, ranking alongside "self-catering" in the catalogue of phrases that repel instead of attract. "Self-catering" should bring to mind the freedom from hotel routine and the benefits of being a family unit doing your own thing on holiday. Instead you think of trailing around foreign supermarkets and spending sunshine hours in the kitchen. So it is with "educational factor". Don't think of education in terms of classrooms and examinations, but rather in the wider sense of broadening the mind, which is what travel traditionally is supposed to do.

You may take a Short Break holiday in Britain and spend the time getting to know more about, let us say, antiques – not because you have to, but because you want to. Though the process is, strictly speaking, educational, the experience is pleasurable and the subsequent benefits can be considerable – spotting an overlooked treasure on the twopenny stall at a local jumble sale being one.

Many hundreds of people are now sampling that kind of holiday experience. Gathering in pleasant company to listen to experts who can help you get more from your hobby or some special interest is a rapidly growing part of the Short Break scene. A glance at any brochure will show how broad that "educational" strand has become. Everything from the aforementioned antique appreciation, through cookery and bridge, to fly-fishing and industrial archaeology by way of sail-training and dancing! Whatever your hobby or interest, there's likely to be a holiday on offer that will appeal.

Talking recently with Reece Gannaway, who handles some of the media and public relations for Trusthouse Forte, I was amazed to discover just how widespread that company's "Country Pursuits" programme has become – and to learn that 1990 marks the 25th anniversary of their "Music at Leisure" weekends. For those seeking musical education in its widest form, this year features such world famous performers as Julian Lloyd-Webber, Moura Lympany, Marisa Robles and the Allegri String Quartet.

"The appealing thing about 'Country Pursuits' is that the breaks can be enjoyed by absolute beginners to a sport or hobby," explained Ms. Gannaway. "But they are just as enjoyable for people who have got beyond the novice stage and want to increase their proficiency."

In previous issues of *Recommended Short Break Holidays in Britain* I have written about the ingredients which I personally look for in the ideal holiday – an hotel with character, good company, the pleasures of dining and wining, and some interesting places to visit in the near vicinity. Perhaps I should now add that "educational factor" to the list, and join that increasing number of people who want to derive an extra benefit from their leisure time. Should I brush up my Shakespeare, or study Gilbert and Sullivan? Try trout fishing, or go for tennis lessons? One thing's for sure – there's no shortage of options for anybody who wants to learn at leisure.

Padstow, North.

CONTENTS

ENGLAND – 'A Review of the Regions'

Southern England 9
South West England 10
East Anglia 11
The Midlands 13
The North of England 15

ENGLAND – County by County

Greater London	17	Leicestershire	75
Avon	19	Greater Manchester	76
Bedfordshire	21	Merseyside	77
Cambridgeshire	22	Norfolk	78
Cheshire	22	Northumberland	81
Cornwall	23	Oxfordshire	83
Cumbria	30	Shropshire	85
Derbyshire	41	Somerset	87
Devon	43	Staffordshire	91
Dorset	54	Suffolk	91
Durham	59	East Sussex	93
Essex	60	West Sussex	97
Gloucestershire	61	Tyne and Wear	99
Hampshire	64	Warwickshire	100
Herefordshire	66	West Midlands	103
Hertfordshire	69	Wiltshire	104
Isle of Wight	70	Worcestershire	105
Kent	71	North Yorkshire	107
Lancashire	73	West Yorkshire	113

WALES

Clwyd	116	Gwent	121
Dyfed	118	Gwynedd	122
South Glamorgan	120	Powys	126

SCOTLAND

Argyll	129	Nairnshire	138
Ayrshire	130	Perthshire	139
Banffshire	131	Ross-shire	141
Edinburgh & Lothians	132	Stirlingshire	142
Fife	135	Wigtownshire	143
Inverness-shire	136	Orkneys	143

Map Section 145

COUNTRY CLUB HOTELS. YOU'LL ENJOY THE EXPERIENCE.

We have created a unique environment at every Country Club Hotel.

Take a break from routine and re-charge your batteries in the relaxing surroundings of our hotels, all with extensive leisure facilities. Ten superb country locations, most with their own golf course, yet within minutes of the motorway system.

Things will look better after a few days away at a Country Club Hotel!

COUNTRY CLUB HOTELS

651 Redwood House, Beggar Bush Lane, Failand, Bristol BS8 3TG
Tel: Bristol (0272) 394000 Telex: 449344 Fax: (0272) 394289.

SOUTHERN ENGLAND

The primary attraction of Southern England is the landscape. Nestling behind the towns and villages are rolling downs, orchards, forest and heaths, while chalk cliffs and shingle combine in a way that is characteristically English.

There are many fine walks to enjoy in what is now common land. Much of Sussex's fame rests on the South Downs where panoramic views can be enjoyed in an area littered with Roman remains.

Between the splendid Martello towers of Kent and Sussex lie the many and varied resorts. Some, such as Brighton, retain their Georgian elegance and splendour while others have taken on the breezy, refreshing look of so many seaside resorts. At the headlands of the Seven Sisters the famous chalk cliffs can be seen to their best advantage while along the coast into Kent the good sands and long hours of sunshine attract visitors to the resorts along the north coast.

Throughout the countryside there is a deep sense of history. Towns like Canterbury retain much of their medieval atmosphere, and the Elizabethan village of Chiddingstone is kept in near perfect condition by the National Trust.

Off the mainland the pretty Isle of Wight delights visitors with its high chalk downs, famous chines and thatched cottages standing in charming villages, while in Hampshire proper, pony trekking is probably the best way to appreciate the famous New Forest, rich in prehistoric remains and landmarks.

If you prefer some city life, look no further than Britain's teeming capital. For a day out or a short break there's probably too much to choose from. Explore the alleyways of the City, visit the Tower close by, and five minutes on the tube will take you to the Houses of Parliament and Westminster.

Spend time shopping in the elegant surroundings of Covent Garden and if it all gets too much escape to the river and take a boat along the Thames to Hampton Court and Greenwich. And if you need something quieter still, the almost rural town of Richmond is nearby with the famous botanic gardens at Kew.

You'll really only get a full picture from local information centres and you should contact Tourist Boards as follows:

East and West Sussex, Kent and Surrey: **The South East England Tourist Board, 1 Warwick Park, Tunbridge Wells, Kent TN2 5TA (Tunbridge Wells [0892] 40766).**

Eastern Dorset, Hampshire, Isle of Wight: **The Southern Tourist Board, 40 Chamberlayne Road, Eastleigh, Hants SO5 5JH (Eastleigh [0703] 620010).**

Bedfordshire, Berkshire, Buckinghamshire, Hertfordshire and Oxfordshire: **The Thames and Chilterns Tourist Board, The Mount House, Church Green, Witney, Oxon OX8 6D2 (0993-778800).**

Greater London: **The London Tourist Board, 26 Grosvenor Gardens, London SW1W 0ET (071-730 9367).**

HOLIDAY ACCOMMODATION Classification Schemes in England, Scotland and Wales

The National Tourist Boards for England, Scotland and Wales have agreed a common 'Crown Classification' scheme for **serviced (Board)** accommodation. All establishments are inspected regularly and are given a classification indicating their level of facilities and services. There are six grades ranging from 'Listed' to 'Five Crowns ♛♛♛♛♛'. The higher the classification, the more facilities and services offered. Crown classification is a measure of *facilities* not *quality*. A common quality grading scheme grades the quality of establishments as 'Approved', 'Commended' or 'Highly Commended' according to the accommodation, welcome and service they provide.

For **Self-Catering**, holiday homes in England are awarded 'Keys' after inspection and can also be 'Approved', 'Commended' or 'Highly Commended' according to the facilities available. In Scotland the Crown scheme includes self-catering accommodation and Wales also has a voluntary inspection scheme for self-catering grading from '1 (Standard)' to '5 (Excellent)'.

Caravan and Camping Parks can participate in the British Holiday Parks grading scheme from 'Approved (√)' to 'Excellent (√ √ √ √)'. In addition, each National Tourist Board has an annual award for high-quality caravan accommodation: in England – Rose Awards; in Scotland – Thistle Commendations; in Wales – Dragon Awards.

When advertisers supply us with the information, FHG Publications show Crowns and other awards or gradings, including AA, RAC, Egon Ronay etc. We also award a small number of Farm Holiday Guide Diplomas every year, based on readers' recommendations.

Southern England 9

SOUTH-WEST ENGLAND

What makes the South-West Britain's most popular holiday region is its warm climate and splendid coastline, but inland too the spectacular moorland scenery, rolling hills, and rich pastoral lands make sure that this is an area with something to offer every kind of holidaymaker.

The traveller from the north should take time to explore the scenery of Gloucestershire, especially the charming town of Chipping Campden, built of honey-coloured Cotswold stone and nestling in the hills. In Somerset relaxation is easily achieved among the old picturesque villages, churches and fine stately homes scattered throughout the green, rolling countryside. If you arrive from the east, don't miss out on the delights of the beautiful county of Dorset, home of Thomas Hardy, which offers an abundance of seaside resorts and pretty towns among the chalk hills.

Moving into the heart of the West Country, the unmistakable quality of Devon is evident from the moment you cross its boundaries. This is a land of striking contrasts, on the coast and inland. The most spectacular scenery lies in the north with magnificent cliffs interspersed with stretches of sandy beach, while the south offers a continental atmosphere of blue skies and golden sands.

Inland lies the rugged desolate beauty of Dartmoor where the buildings of prehistoric man are still visible in a landscape inhabited only by the famous Dartmoor ponies.

Visitors to the Duchy of Cornwall should make the most of a visit by touring round the countryside. This is a marine county with the sea never more than 20 miles away. In the north the air is exhilarating and the savage headlands of the coastline most striking.

Several of the county's most popular resorts are set along the sheltered harbours of the coast: Newquay, St. Agnes and St. Ives are probably among the most visited each year. The southern climate is milder, allowing tropical plants and palm trees to grow among a luxuriantly coloured landscape.

During your visit take a trip along the coast or over to the lovely Scilly Isles or sample the atmosphere of a true Cornish village at Polperro with its lime-washed houses set in steep lanes.

For further information about Avon, Cornwall, Devon, Somerset, Western Dorset, Wiltshire and the Isles of Scilly contact: **The West Country Tourist Board, Trinity Court, Southernhay East, Exeter EX1 1QS (Exeter [0392] 76351).**

Newquay Harbour.

10   South-West England

Take a Break in EAST ANGLIA

Much of East Anglia is still waiting to be discovered. Bordering London to the south, the region is still a place of hushed forests, reed fringed waterways and windswept sand dunes.

And yet East Anglia is a place of many contrasts. Essex, with its busy towns, is full of white-painted weatherboard villages and winding river estuaries. And who would think, in the leafy shade of Epping Forest, that London is less than 20 miles away. Colchester is England's oldest recorded town, with a Norman castle built on the foundations of a Roman temple, still showing the scars of Civil War battles, and a busy new shopping centre. Maldon is the home port for many sailing barges. Take a walk along Hythe quay and admire the barges with their tan sails and down-to-earth names like *Kitty* or *Ironsides*. John Constable loved the countryside on the Essex/Suffolk borders. Visitors to Constable Country can see views almost unchanged since Constable's time.

The most famous of Suffolk's "Wool" towns is fabulous timbered Lavenham – England's best preserved medieval town. Ipswich, the county town and an important port since Saxon times, is a busy port, commercial and shopping centre. Newmarket is the centre of the British horse breeding and racing industry. Strings of elegant horses clatter through the town on their way to the Heath and the High Street shops are full of riding gear and horsey books. East Anglia's 200 mile coastline is particularly charming in Suffolk. Resorts like Felixstowe and Lowestoft have a traditional appeal, while Aldeburgh and Southwold are pretty little seaside towns with pastel washed cottages and pebbly beaches.

Norfolk's biggest resort is Great Yarmouth, with miles of sandy beaches and every entertainment you can think of. Cromer is a bustling little resort mixing Victorian red brick with traditional Norfolk flint. Fishermen's boats are drawn up on the beach and the lifeboat is always ready. Inland, the city of Norwich is full of surprises. Narrow medieval streets reveal specialist shops, courtyards and lanes running down to the river. One of Norfolk's most famous areas is the Broads, where over 200 miles of navigable waterways provide everyone with the opportunity to get afloat. Although busy and full of fun in the summer, it is still possible to find tree fringed Broads where you can enjoy the sunset with only the swans for company.

A day's visit is hardly long enough to discover all that Cambridge has to offer. The shopping is all that you would expect, with an extraordinary variety of bookshops. The colleges are truly marvellous, you can go punting or rowing on the river, take a guided tour, or visit the museums and art galleries. Drive across the flat, fertile black land of the Fens and on the horizon you will see the massive presence of Ely cathedral dominating the skyline. Ely's mellow stone buildings cluster round the skirts of the cathedral whose Lantern Tower is a masterpiece of medieval engineering using mighty oak trees sixty feet high.

Conkers, plump and shiny as the Queen's carriage horses; pagan lines of fire leaping and flaring across stubble fields in the autumn dusk; young voices piercing the December sky over King's College Chapel; woods crowded with daffodils – there are so many good reasons to visit East Anglia in autumn, winter or spring. What could be more lovely than the cherry blossom around the cathedral in Norwich, or Cambridge with the Bridge of Sighs delicately traced with snow, or Thetford Forest bright with bracken? A short break is the perfect opportunity to leave behind the pressures of your everyday life and take some time to stand and stare.

But you won't be bored. There's lots to do if you've got the energy. You'll catch the beginning and end of the flat racing season at Newmarket, steeplechasing and point-to-points, the Norwich Jazz and Beer Festivals, Santa Specials at the Colne and Nene Valley Railways, Bungay Street Fair, the ancient January tradition of the Whittlesey

Straw Bear, the Shire Horse Show, Daffodil Days and Primrose Festivals, farm open days to see the newborn lambs.

All our great National Trust houses are open in autumn and spring and many attractions are open all year round. Country parks, museums, steam railways, gardens, vineyards and windmills – all welcome visitors at this time of year. Or how about Sacrewell Watermill, Farm and Country Centre near Peterborough where you can touch and work anything from a 1920's egg whisk to a turn of the century rotavator? Or the Ada Cole Memorial Stables near Harlow, where you can see rescued horses, ponies, donkeys and mules. The University of Cambridge Botanic Garden, right in the city centre, is fascinating, and so is Brookcroft Bunnery near Royston with hundreds of rabbits and a shop selling angora knitwear. Norfolk Lavender near Hunstanton is open all year, and you can walk underwater without getting wet at the Sealife Centres at Hunstanton and Great Yarmouth. At Aspall Cider near Stowmarket in Suffolk, you can see a 1728 cider press, and the Dunwich Underwater Exploration Exhibition tells the story of the medieval city under the sea. Stand on the stoney beach and listen for the sound of the sunken church bells over the roar of winter waves!

For more details on What to Do and Where to Go in the counties of Cambridge, Essex, Norfolk and Suffolk, contact: **The East Anglia Tourist Board, Toppesfield Hall, Hadleigh, Suffolk IP7 5DN (Hadleigh [0473] 822922).**

NEW WORLD HOTEL
Great Warley Street, Warley, Brentwood
Tel: 0277 226418/220483   Fax: 0277 229795

"3 minutes from M25"

A Tudor-style manor house situated in the heart of the undulating Essex countryside, within 3 minutes of London Orbital Motorway.
Well appointed refurbished bedrooms – each with colour TV and telephone; *Shower in every room; *Valet trouser press; *Tea & coffee making facilities; *12 acres of garden; *Heated pool; *2 brand new tennis courts.
Enquire for our Special Weekend Rates.
WE ARE THE BEST VALUE IN ESSEX.

PUBLISHER'S NOTE

While every effort is made to ensure accuracy, we regret that FHG Publications cannot accept responsibility for errors, omissions or misrepresentation in our entries or any consequences thereof. Prices in particular should be checked because we go to press early. We will follow up complaints but cannot act as arbiters or agents for either party.

THE MIDLANDS
Contrasts and Surprises in the Heart of England

The *Heart of England* is a name which suggests that here you will find all that we like to think of as traditional rural England. At the very centre of England, the Heart of England can be reached easily by motorway in only a few hours from any part of Britain, and it is a region well worth exploring: from the Cotswolds with their own timeless charm to the wild, dramatic moorlands of Staffordshire and the peace and tranquillity of the western border counties.

At the northern edge of the Cotswolds is Stratford-upon-Avon, famous as the birthplace of William Shakespeare. You can visit any of half a dozen houses associated with him, see his tomb in the lovely parish church, or enjoy one of his plays performed by the world famous Royal Shakespeare Company in their theatres on the banks of the River Avon.

If you really want to escape, head west and make your own personal discoveries. Perhaps to Herefordshire and the lovely Wye Valley, or further north to Shropshire – both counties are bordered by the Welsh Marches where England meets Wales, the scene of many past bloody battles. Here the countryside quickly changes from the small rural villages and market towns to wild hill-land dotted with ancient castles and fortified manor houses. There are few large hotels but any amount of country inns – often old black and white timbered buildings which have provided accommodation and simple food for centuries – and miles and miles of empty roads through fruit orchards and rich pastoral countryside where you scarcely meet a soul.

The Heart of England has a wealth of places to visit. On a larger scale than the many ruined castles and fortresses is the superbly preserved Warwick Castle, dominating the Avon a few miles north of Stratford. The home of the Earls of Warwick for a thousand years, it is the finest medieval castle in England. Nearby are the romantic ruins of Kenilworth Castle where Queen Elizabeth I was the guest on several occasions of Robert, Earl of Leicester. Another castle with royal connections is Sudeley near Cheltenham, the last home of Catherine Parr, the one wife who outlived Henry VIII.

There are many stately homes of special interest which are open to the public. Ragley Hall, near Stratford, is the home of the Marquess of Hertford. It is a Palladian house with a magnificent Great Hall which has some of the finest baroque plasterwork in England. Weston Park is on the Shropshire/Staffordshire border. The home of the Earl of Bradford, it is a superb Restoration house with a treasury of tapestry and furniture and a noted art collection. Both houses have attractions for children and lovely parklands where wild animals roam. Hagley Hall, opened to the public by Viscount Cobham, is also a Palladian house with beautiful Italian plasterwork, a fine art collection of paintings and wonderful landscaped parklands. It is just south of Birmingham, Britain's 'second city'.

From the famous mansions of earlier times, the mind turns easily to beautiful gardens and parklands. Especially memorable are the rose gardens at Hidcote Manor and the collections at Burford House not far from Ludlow, and at Hergest Croft high up on Hergest Ridge looking towards Wales. The Botanical Gardens in Birmingham are a haven of peace and beauty so close to the city centre, and autumn sees the Arboreta at Westonbirt and Batsford turning more vivid hues than you could have imagined.

There are also conservation centres for rare breeds of animals. The Cotswold Farm Park, for instance, has dozens of rare breeds of farm animals, while Peter Scott's Wildfowl Trust at Slimbridge is a sanctuary for birds from all over the world who migrate each year to the open sand flats of the River Severn.

In a region of contrasts, perhaps one of the greatest is Alton Towers, Europe's premier leisure park. Beautiful landscaped gardens and a ruined stately home are the setting for a Disney-style playground with over 80 attractions for old and young alike. Staffordshire also contrasts town and country. Miles of moorlands and dramatic landscapes surround Stoke-on-Trent, better known as The Potteries, and today offering a fascinating visitor experience with its wealth of famous china factories and award-winning museums.

The Heart of England is the setting for many famous festivals. The Three Choirs, the oldest musical festival in the world, is staged in alternate years in the beautiful cathedral cities of Worcester, Gloucester and Hereford. Malvern has an annual festival based around the theatrical works of George Bernard Shaw and the music of Edward Elgar. At Cheltenham there are international festivals of music and literature, Shrewsbury has a poetry festival and International Flower Show, and Ludlow Festival offers Shakespeare in the open air – with the perfect theatrical backdrop of the castle ruins. Still out of doors, in Coventry, ancient mystery plays enacting the life of Christ are performed in the haunting shell of the bombed cathedral, while at Stratford there is a programme of events and performances throughout the town, with something for everyone.

Altogether, a region of surprises and contrasts. If your holiday doesn't depend on the seaside and you want to discover the lesser known but very beautiful parts of rural England, then this is a region to discover.

Further north and west you'll find Staffordshire with its moorlands cutting into the stark scenery of the Peak District which includes the potteries of current and historical interest and the graceful cathedral of Lichfield. Shropshire contrasts the industrial heritage of Ironbridge with the Welsh border uplands and the upper Severn valley. Ludlow, Bridgnorth and Shrewsbury are excellent centres.

There are few stately homes more impressive than Chatsworth, on the edge of Derbyshire's Peak District whose rocky moorlands contrast strongly with the flat stretches of Lincolnshire and the Wash.

For more comprehensive information about the Midlands you should contact the Tourist Boards as follows:

Gloucester, Hereford & Worcester, Shropshire, Staffordshire, Warwickshire and West Midlands: **The Heart of England Tourist Board, the Trinity, 2-4 Trinity Street, Worcester WR1 2PW (Worcester [0905] 613132 and 29512).**

Derbyshire, Leicestershire, Lincolnshire, Northamptonshire and Nottinghamshire: **The East Midlands Tourist Board, Exchequergate, Lincoln LN2 1PZ (Lincoln [0522] 531521).**

Chatsworth House and Bridge, Derbyshire.

14 *Midlands*

THE NORTH OF ENGLAND
East, West, the Lakes and Isle of Man

The scenic jewel of the North is, of course, the Lake District, a magnet for tourists with its 16 major lakes surrounded by the Cumbrian Mountains. At 866 square miles it is the largest National Park in the country, but despite the popularity of the place the walker can still find solitude among the hills and valleys. The most popular centres for touring are Keswick and Windermere, but there are dozens of little towns and villages to choose from as a base for exploration.

Along the coast the best resorts are to be found around Morecambe Bay and the Fylde coast. Morecambe is the region's most northerly and most popular seaside resort. Further south is the lovely fishing village of Fleetwood, linked by tram to its larger-than-life neighbour, Blackpool, the best known resort of this area with every imaginable holiday entertainment.

And don't be put off by the reputation of the industrial towns of Wigan, Bolton and Burnley, now enjoying a comeback in the celebration of their industrial heritage, while Chester, with its half-timbered Tudor houses, is definitely worth a visit. The city of Manchester stages first class drama and opera, and its Free Trade Hall houses the famous Halle Orchestra.

By way of contrast, take the ferry from Liverpool to the independent sovereignty of the Isle of Man. The climate is mild, warmed by the Gulf Stream, and the clear sea is perfect for scuba-diving. There are some excellent walks along wild, wooded glens – and if you want to take it easy use the mountain railway to the top of Snaefell or just relax along the 100 miles of silvery sands.

The North-East boasts some of the most beautiful and unspoilt scenery in England. Visitors can rediscover peace and solitude in the wild, desolate moorlands of Northumbria or the remote hillsides of the North York Moors, while the more energetic walker will enjoy the challenge of the Pennine Way. But this is an area to explore not only for the stunning natural beauty of the landscape: the graceful ruins of monastic houses, fine stately homes, Norman castles and magnificent Cistercian abbeys rest in the lush dales just waiting for the tourist who doesn't mind straying off the beaten track, while the best preserved sections of Hadrian's Wall are to be found at Housesteads, near Hexham, in the Northumbrian National Park.

There's plenty to see in the towns and villages too, from picturesque Romaldskirk and Blanchford and the delightful eighteenth-century houses and inns of the town of Yarm, to the grander delights of Durham, with its magnificent Norman castle and cathedral, and elegant York, offering a prestigious cultural heritage within its medieval walls.

If you just want to relax on an uncrowded sandy beach you could do no better than the long white sandy shores of the Northumbrian coast where the spectacular cliff scenery and sheltered coves are now protected by the National Trust. Further south, Scarborough, Filey and Whitley Bay offer more in the way of popular entertainment, while the charming fishing village of Robin Hood's Bay and Berwick-upon-Tweed cater for those with quieter tastes.

These are all superb Short Break locations and the local Tourist Boards can supply more detailed information and assistance, as follows:

Cleveland, Durham, Northumberland, Tyne & Wear: **The Northumbria Tourist Board, Aykley Heads, Durham DH1 5UX (Durham [091-384] 3720).**

Cumbria: **The Cumbria Tourist Board, Ashleigh, Holly Road, Windermere, Cumbria LA23 2AQ (Windermere [096-62] 4444).**

Cheshire, Greater Manchester, Lancashire, Merseyside: **The North West Tourist Board, The Last Drop Village, Bromley Cross, Bolton BL7 9PZ (Bolton [0204] 591511).**

North, South and West Yorkshire, Humberside: **The Yorkshire and Humberside Tourist Board, 312 Tadcaster Road, York YO2 2HF (York [0904] 707961).**

The Isle of Man Tourist Board, 13 Victoria Street, Douglas, Isle of Man (0624 74323).

Publisher's Note

At the start of some counties you will see Display advertisements for accommodation.

Each of these advertisers also has a standard entry in the main classified section under the appropriate town.

EXPLANATION OF SYMBOLS

TA	Travel Agency Commission
♛	Number of Crowns
?	Number of Keys
🐕	Pets Welcome
🐎	Reductions for Children
♿	Suitable for Disabled
🌲	Christmas Breaks

The symbols are arranged in the same order throughout the book so that looking down each page will give a quick comparison.

ENGLAND – County by County

Greater London

ABBEY COURT HOTEL
174 Sussex Gardens, London W2 1TP
071-402 0704 Fax: 071-224 9114

TA

A central London hotel which has been newly furbished and offers good accommodation at moderate rates. It is only two minutes from Hyde Park and from Lancaster Gate and Paddington tube stations, and is near bus routes. There is a pleasant and friendly atmosphere throughout, and all bedrooms are comfortable, with central heating, radio/intercom, and washbasins in every room. Most also have private showerrooms and colour TV, and there is a television lounge. Children are most welcome. £ *Single from £16, double from £13.50, bed and breakfast per person, depending on season. Discounts available on normal prices for periods of stay exceeding three days.* ☺ *All year.*

SASS HOUSE HOTEL
11 Craven Terrace, London W2 3QD
071-262 2325 Fax: 071-224 9114

Good, clean accommodation is offered in this centrally situated hotel, within walking distance of Hyde Park, Oxford Street, and Marble Arch. Paddington and Lancaster Gate tube stations are nearby, and the area is served by a network of buses to all places of interest. Rooms are comfortable – all are centrally heated, with radio and intercom fitted. There is a colour television lounge. Parking is available for guests' cars.

£ *Single from £16, double from £11, bed and breakfast per person, depending on season and facilities. Special reductions for three-day minimum stays if booked in advance.* ☺ *All year.*

Greater London   17

WESTPOINT HOTEL
170 Sussex Gardens, London W2 1TP
071-402 0281 Fax: 071-224 9114

A pleasant hotel centrally located in a tree lined avenue close to Hyde Park and served by Paddington and Lancaster Gate tube stations and several bus routes. Westpoint offers good accommodation at reasonable prices. Many of the rooms have private facilities, and most have colour television. There is also a colour television lounge. Parking for guests' cars. There are many tourist attractions in easy reach, including Hyde Park, the West End, and Oxford Street.

£ *Single from £15, double from £11, bed and breakfast per person, depending on season. Special discount on normal rates for breaks of three days or more.* All year.

HOTEL SLAVIA
2 Pembridge Square, London W2
071-727 1316

Modernised family run hotel, in Victorian garden square just off the Bayswater Road and a mere 200 metres from an underground station served by three main lines. The Portobello Antique Market is located round the corner and there are good bus services, therefore the majority of London's attractions are a mere 10 minutes or so away. Most of the 31 bedrooms are en suite with showers and WC and have telephones. Colour TV lounge.

£ *£31-£34 per night for double/twin room. Single supplement. Rates include VAT and continental breakfast. Minimum stay of 2 nights.* 1 November to 31 March low season; 1 April to 31 October high season.

EXPLANATION OF SYMBOLS

TA	Travel Agency Commission
♕	Number of Crowns
♀	Number of Keys
🐕	Pets Welcome
🎠	Reductions for Children
♿	Suitable for Disabled
🎄	Christmas Breaks

The symbols are arranged in the same order throughout the book so that looking down each page will give a quick comparison.

Avon

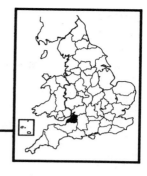

BAILBROOK LODGE HOTEL
35/37 London Road West, Bath BA1 7HZ
0225 859090

Bailbrook Lodge is a splendid Georgian hotel overlooking the magnificent Avon Valley. AA and RAC **. All bedrooms have shower or bathroom en suite, television and tea/coffee making facilities. It is fully licensed. Bath is without doubt one of Britain's most beautiful cities, with a wealth of historical and literary associations. Bailbrook Lodge is ideal for touring the Cotswold villages, Longleat, Stourhead, Bowood House and many other places of interest.

£ *£55 per person for 2 nights dinner, bed and breakfast (four-poster beds extra). Extra nights pro rata.*
1st October to 31st March (except Christmas).

BROMPTON HOUSE HOTEL
St John's Road, Bath
0225 420972

TA

An elegant Georgian rectory set in beautiful secluded gardens, Brompton House has been extensively modernised while still retaining most of its original Georgian features. A chance to relax and unwind in tranquil surroundings is offered here. AA recommended; RAC highly acclaimed. Bedrooms are en suite with colour TV, and a choice of traditional English food or a wholefood breakfast is offered every morning. Ideal for a break in the beautiful city of Bath, being only a few minutes' level walk to the city centre. Licensed. Car park.

£ *From £50 per person for 2 nights sharing double/twin room en suite, plus breakfast. 1 January to 23 December.*

LANSDOWN GROVE HOTEL
Lansdown Road, Bath BA1 5EH
0225 315891

TA

A three star hotel in its own grounds in the beautiful city of Bath. All bedrooms have private facilities, telephone, colour television, and tea and coffee makers. Mini-bar. AA***. Excellent food is served in the restaurant, and guests can relax with an aperitif or after-dinner drink in the comfortable bar. There is much to see and do in Bath, and many sports — including ballooning — can be arranged nearby. Convenient for the Roman Baths, Theatre Royal, Carriage Museum, Wookey Hole, and Longleat.

£ *From £41 – £46 per person per night for dinner, bed and breakfast. All year.*

THE CLIFFE HOTEL
Crowe Hill, Lower Limpley Stoke, Bath BA3 6HY
0225 723226 Fax: 0225 723871

With panoramic views across the beautiful Avon Valley, this lovely country house has three acres of terraced grounds and a reputation for superb food, wine and service. AA***. Great care and imagination has gone into the furnishings and guests' rooms are fully equipped to the most exacting modern standards. It boasts a beautiful four poster bedroom and superior rooms with whirlpool bath en suite. The hotel is quietly situated in the country, yet just minutes by car from Bath and many other places of interest.

[£] *"Getaway" Breaks, minimum 2 nights stay, from £116 per couple per night for dinner, bed and breakfast. "Romantic" Breaks: from £140 per couple per night.* ☐ *February – December.*

THE OLD MILL HOTEL & RESTAURANT
Tollbridge Road, Batheaston, Bath BA1 7DE
0225 858476

This luxurious hotel, situated five minutes from the city centre, is magnificently set on the banks of the Avon. Most of the en suite bedrooms have breathtaking river views and all have colour TV and telephone; some have four-poster beds. RAC**. Delicious cuisine is served in the Riverside à la carte Restaurant and interesting and varied meals and business lunches are available in the fully licensed bar.

[£] *Single from £45, double from £55 for 2, bed and English breakfast, depending on season.*

THE OLD SCHOOL HOUSE
Church Street, Bathford, Bath BA1 7RR
0225 859593

This charming early Victorian schoolhouse is set in the conservation area of the pretty, walled village of Bathford, with views over the Avon Valley. Bath city centre is just three miles away. Tourist Board Commended. AA Selected. All rooms, including two ground floor rooms suitable for the less mobile, have private bathrooms and full amenities including colour TV and telephone. The hotel is licensed, with winter log fires and candlelit dinners. At this small NO SMOKING hotel we aim to offer friendly personal service in an informal country house setting.

[£] *Special Breaks: £60 per person for two weekdays dinner, bed and breakfast. £65 weekends. Extra nights £25 p.p. These rates based on two persons sharing a double room.* ☐ *October to March.*

WENTWORTH HOUSE HOTEL
106 Bloomfield Road, Bath BA2 2AP
0225 339193

Traditional bed and breakfast in comfortable imposing Victorian house set in large gardens within walking distance of the Roman Baths and Abbey. The diningroom has a conservatory which overlooks the garden and outdoor swimming pool which is open in the summer. Large car park. There are 20 comfortable bedrooms, some with private bath or shower. All rooms have tea/coffee making facilities and telephones. Excellent base for touring. Licensed. AA Listed, RAC Acclaimed.

[£] *Double or twin rooms £17 to £24 per person per night, including full English breakfast.*

CHELWOOD HOUSE HOTEL
Chelwood BS18 4NH
0761 490730

The recipe for a memorable short break. RAC***, AA**. A 300 year old house redolent of yesteryear's elegance and charm inside, and surrounded by nature's excellent work outside. The jewel in the triangle, Chelwood House is situated almost equidistant from Bath, Bristol and Wells. Beautiful en suite bedrooms with either draped beds or four-posters of different styles, colour TV and telephone. Privately owned and personally supervised by the Chef Proprietor. A delightful new 'Restaurant in a Garden'. A conservatory-type dining room with a garden ambience.
£ *Dinner, bed and breakfast for 2 nights £107 per person sharing room.* ☐ *All year.*

WALTON PARK HOTEL
Wellington Terrace, Clevedon BS21 7BL
0272 874253

Set in a spectacular position above the Severn Estuary, the Walton Park is a fine Victorian hotel enjoying excellent views from the bar, restaurant and the majority of its spacious bedrooms. AA/RAC***. The setting is perfect yet only 2 miles from Junction 20 of the M5 and 12 miles from Bristol. It is ideal for both business people and visitors. Local attractions include Clevedon Court and Cheddar Gorge and regular sailings on the paddle steamers *Waverley* and *Balmoral* leave from Clevedon Pier. The hotel has 5 conference rooms accommodating from 10-150 delegates and has ample parking. Call for a copy of our brochure.
£ *From £83 per person for 2 nights bed, breakfast and dinner.* ☐ *All year except Christmas.*

Bedfordshire

THE SWAN HOTEL AND RESTAURANT
High Street, Leighton Buzzard LU7 7EA
0525 372148

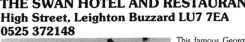

This famous Georgian coaching inn dates back to the 18th century and was once used as a coach posting stop between Oxford and Cambridge. It has been stylishly redeveloped, while retaining its traditional character, all the individually designed bedrooms having private facilities and all the comforts expected from a top hotel. AA/RAC***, Michelin, Egon Ronay, Good Food Guide. Leighton Buzzard is a charming market town with much to offer the visitor, including a very fine restored medieval church. Good central location, close to M1 and A5, and many places of interest in the area.
£ *Friday, Saturday, Sunday — £37.50 per person dinner, room and breakfast, based on 2 persons sharing, minimum stay 2 nights.* ☐ *All year except Christmas.*

Avon/Bedfordshire 21

Cambridgeshire

QUY MILL HOTEL
Newmarket Road, Quy, Cambridge CB5 9AG
0223 853383

A friendly country house hotel with unique heritage set in 14 acres of gardens. Only three miles from Cambridge, and within easy reach of Newmarket, Anglesey Abbey, RAF museum at Duxford, Ely Cathedral, and nature reserves. All bedrooms are en suite and all have TV, telephone, and tea/coffee making facilities. The restaurant specialises in high quality home made food and an extensive range of bar meals is also available. Plenty to do including fishing and walking. We welcome animals and have our own kennels.

£ **£55 per person for two nights bed and breakfast, dinner optional.** All year.

Cheshire

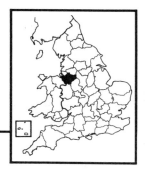

THE EATON HOTEL
City Road, Chester CH1 3AE
0244 320840

The Eaton Hotel is the perfect central location, equidistant between station, River Dee, Roman Walls and main shops — all within a few minutes' stroll. You will find that the Eaton Hotel, with its delightful restaurant and bar lounge and the advantage of parking on the premises, is the ideal base for sightseeing in the city of Chester. All rooms have bath or shower (most with WC also), colour television, radio, telephone, hairdryers and tea making facilities.

£ **£49 (shower only), £54 (en suite) for any two nights dinner, bed and breakfast. Rates are per person sharing room.** Until end March 1991. Short breaks available all summer.

Cornwall

THE WELLINGTON HOTEL
The Harbour, Boscastle PL35 0AQ
08405 202

Commended

Historic, listed 16th century Coaching Inn of real character. Set in glorious National Trust country by Elizabethan Harbour. Very comfortable, 21 bedrooms (16 en suite), full central heating, direct-dial telephones, four-poster bed, colour TVs, tea/coffee making. Excellent Anglo-French Georgian restaurant plus Freehouse with real ales and buffet. Lots of atmosphere, log fires, beams and real hospitality. Antiques and Wellingtonia on display. 10 acres private woodland walks. Pets always welcome. Write or phone for free brochure. *AA/RAC ***.

£ *Terms on application.*

16th Century
Jubilee Inn

PELYNT
NEAR LOOE
CORNWALL

TEL: 0503 20312

Comfortable and spacious 400-year-old inn, situated on the Looe/Lostwithiel road, just 2 miles from the sea. All the attractively furnished rooms are ensuite, with colour TV and central heating. The attractive gardens and lawns include a barbecue area and a safe children's play area. Wholesome English food is served in the restaurant, which is famed for its seafood dishes.

Special Short Break Terms (3-6 nights) £31.50 per person per night for Dinner, Bed and Breakfast.   **AA RAC ★★**

Ashley Courtenay recommended AA**
Watergate Bay, Near Newquay, Cornwall TR8 4AB
Telephone (0637) 860280

100 yards from this glorious sandy beach and spectacular Atlantic coastline.
Peaceful position between Newquay and Padstow.

- ★ 27 rooms, most en suite, all with radio/listening, tea makers, heaters, colour TV available
- ★ Heated pool and sun patio, games room, solarium, sauna and jacuzzi
- ★ Parties and coaches by arrangement
- ★ Spring and Autumn breaks
- ★ Family run; children welcome at reduced rates (some free offers)
- ★ Licensed bar
- ★ Central for touring all of Cornwall
- ★ Open Easter to November

Dinner, bed and breakfast £110 to £200 inclusive
Brochure from resident proprietors Marian and Derrick Molloy

WESTERINGS
Forrabury, Boscastle PL35 0DJ
08405 389

Westerings is a Georgian rectory, peacefully situated close to National Trust headland above the picturesque harbourside village of Boscastle. The one/two bedroom apartments and the two-bedroom bungalows are all fully equipped, with modern kitchens, colour TV, radio and comfortable suites. This is an ideal location for walking and touring, with beaches close by. Pets are welcome at no extra charge and there is a common for walking dogs. All units are heated; linen is available on hire; cot and high chair available. Games room. For further details and brochure contact Shirley Wakelin. ETB Approved.

£ *Short breaks available out of summer season.*

MAER LODGE HOTEL
Crooklets Beach, Bude
0288 353306

Maer Lodge faces south near Crooklets Beach and enjoys peaceful surroundings and a splendid view. There are 20 bedrooms, 16 en suite, and all with TV and tea/coffee facilities. Other amenities include a cocktail bar, TV room, large lounge, pool table and games room. For guests' entertainment there is a Hammond organ and a resident pianist. There is a putting green and an 18-hole golf course just 100 yards away. Brochure on request with tariff and menu guide. AA/RAC*.

£ *Dinner, bed and breakfast from £25-£30 daily inc. VAT.*

MORNISH HOTEL
Summerleaze Crescent, Bude
0288 352972

The Mornish Hotel is situated in the best position in Bude, with magnificent sea views and only two minutes from all amenities. Les Routiers — the sign of good value. All the well furnished bedrooms have en suite facilities and television. The hotel is centrally heated throughout. There is a residents' bar, and good food is served in the attractive diningroom. Pets are welcome, and there are reductions for children. There is ample parking for guests.

£ *£60 for a three-day break with dinner, bed and breakfast. Weekly terms £138.30 including VAT.*
September to May inclusive.

DOUBLEBOIS PARK
Dobwalls, Near Liskeard PL14 6LD
0579 20049 Fax: 0579 21415

Exclusive development of quality timber holiday lodges set in over 60 acres of park and woodland, with its own 9-hole golf course and tennis court. Liskeard is 3 miles away and the picturesque fishing villages of Looe and Polperro about 20 minutes' drive, making this an ideal base for exploring the Cornish Riviera. The lodges are of varying sizes to accommodate from 4 to 7 persons, and are fully equipped, including electricity, colour TV, fridge, microwave and linen. No pets allowed.

£ *Short breaks from 3 days available. Terms on request.* *April to December.*

MELVILLE HOTEL
Sea View Road, Falmouth TR3 6JG
0326 312134

Originally the home of a successful merchant sea captain, the Melville Hotel is attractively set in two acres of sub-tropical gardens overlooking Falmouth Bay and in a convenient situation for the beaches and town centre. AA**, Ashley Courtenay. All the well appointed bedrooms have private facilities, and at the Melville we promise good food, service, and hospitality. Croquet and putting can be played in the garden, while a special feature for short break guests is free membership of Falmouth Club for tennis, squash, table tennis, snooker, billiards, and bridge.
£ *From £92 for three-day bargain break with dinner, bed and breakfast.* *All year.*

TREGILDRY HOTEL
Gillan, Manaccan, Helston TR12 6HG
032-623 378

Staying at Tregildry is like staying at a friend's country home; warmly welcomed by the Norton family who will show you to your comfortable room (all have bathroom en suite and splendid views), guests are then free to wander the four acres of grounds and explore the footpath leading to the cove below. The private access makes it reasonably safe to leave dinghies on the beach here and boat hire and moorings can be arranged. Deservedly enjoying a growing reputation for excellent cuisine. Bar meals are available and the restaurant offers table d'hôte menus. AA, RAC**.
£ *3 night breaks from £115.* *Easter to June and September to mid-October.*

HARESCOMBE LODGE
Watergate, Near Looe PL13 2NE
05036 3158

Once the shooting lodge of the Trelawne Estate, Harescombe Lodge has been tastefully restored to offer luxury accommodation. All bedrooms are en suite, with tea-making facilities and central heating. AA listed. Situated in its own lovely grounds, the Lodge offers peace and tranquillity yet is only a few minutes from Looe and Polperro and the beautiful South Cornwall coast. This is an ideal area for fishing, golf, riding and walking. Full English Breakfast is served, and optional Dinner, using fresh local produce. Regret, no children under 12. Open all year, and ideal for out-of-season breaks.
£ *Bed and breakfast with private bathroom from £13.50 per person per night (Oct. to April), from £15.50 (May to Sept.).*

JUBILEE INN
Pelynt, Near Looe PL13 2JZ
0503 20312

This 400-year-old inn, situated on the Looe-Lostwithiel road, is attractively furnished throughout, all rooms having private facilities, colour TV and central heating. AA/RAC**. Wholesome English food is served in the restaurant, which is famed for its seafood dishes. Attractive gardens and lawns include a barbecue area and a safe children's play area – ideal for parents relaxing with a drink or a snack. The village of Pelynt is situated 2 miles from the sea, convenient for sailing, boating, bathing and fishing. Local places of interest include a theme park and an animal farm.
£ *3-6 days dinner, bed and breakfast £31.50 per person per night.* ❐ *All year.*

NEWQUAY HOLIDAY MOTEL
Porth, Near Newquay

Ideally situated in own grounds in a peaceful valley about one mile from Newquay. One, two and three roomed suites available, all with private bathrooms, colour TV and tea/coffee facilities. Ample parking space. Newquay overlooks many fine beaches and is a major centre for surfing. Sea fishing, water sports, riding, sports centre, golf, variety theatre, zoo/animal park, bowls and swimming pools. Newquay Holiday Motel is ideal for the exploration of Cornwall, with its coves and caves, harbours and fishing villages, country lanes and woodlands. For bookings contact: Grosvenor House, 20 St Andrews Crescent, Cardiff CF1 3DD (0222 387070 Fax: 0222 223692).
£ *3-day breaks from £55, including suite, English breakfast and evening meal.* ❐ *March to October.*

ALEXANDRA HOTEL
Seafront, Penzance TR18 4NX
0736 62644

A modernised family-run Victorian hotel enjoying glorious views over Mount's Bay. AA*. All bedrooms are en suite, and all have colour TV, radio, telephone, tea making facilities, and central heating. Lounge, licensed bar, launderette, and sun terrace. The restaurant enjoys a good reputation for the quality of its food and service. Tennis, fishing, squash, bowls, and a swimming pool are all available nearby, while Land's End, St. Ives, and The Lizard all lie within easy reach.
£ *2 nights en suite room, breakfast and 4-course dinner from £50-£57.50. Extra nights pro rata.*
❐ *October 1 1990 to 25 May 1991 (excl. Christmas and New Year). Special Christmas and New Year packages.*

CLAREMONT HOTEL
Fore Street, Polperro PL13 2RG
0503 72241

Built around a 17th century cottage, the Claremont overlooks a valley, in the heart of south Cornwall's most picturesque fishing village. It has its own private car park, the traffic being otherwise restricted in the village. Ideally located for walking, golf, swimming, fishing and touring. All rooms have tea-making facilities and colour TV; lounge bar with warm, friendly atmosphere. AA/RAC*. From home-made shepherd's pie to an exclusive French menu, the kitchen caters for every taste and appetite. Ideal for a relaxing holiday, taking advantage of generous discounts for short and longer breaks.
£ *From £32 per person for 2 days bed and breakfast (October to March), from £50 to £60 for 2 days bed, breakfast and dinner (April to September).* All year.

GREENBANK HOLIDAY FLATS
Porth, Newquay TR7 3LW
0637 872546

Greenbank is detached, standing in a large lawned garden within 270 yards of Porth's sandy beach. The flats are fully equipped, carpeted and furnished for two to six persons, with colour TV, fridge, electric cooker, and razor point. Hot water included in tariff. Suitable for couples and families, with cots and high chairs supplied. Laundry room with automatic washing machine and tumble dryer. Guests' telephone. Car park. Personally supervised by resident proprietors. Stamp for brochure. WCTB member.

£ *From £45 according to size of flat and season.* All year.

GLENEGLOS HOTEL
Trewint Lane, Rock PL27 6LU
0208 862369

The aims of Pauline and Mick Burton are a warm, friendly atmosphere with personal service. Their small country style hotel is comfortably furnished with en suite facilities. All bedrooms have television, tea/coffee making facilities, intercom and baby listening device. Freshly prepared meals in the traditional diningroom are complemented by a wide range of wines. The 'Olde Worlde' bar is comfortably furnished for you to enjoy an aperitif and a relaxing drink after your meal.

£ *From £30 per person per day for bed, breakfast and dinner.* February to December.

DRIFTWOOD SPARS HOTEL
Trevaunance Cove, St Agnes TR5 0RT
087-255 2428

Sample some proper Cornish hospitality! Have a lie-in with morning tea and breakfast TV — come down to an enormous breakfast, then laze on the beach or explore the numerous inland and coastal footpaths. Come home and over-indulge in good home cooking, then have a natter with the locals in a choice of two 'timeless' bars. All rooms have colour TV, as well as hairdryers and tea/coffee facilities. Sea-fishing, surfing, swimming, walking all available locally. Please phone for details of our informal holidays.

£ *5 nights bed, breakfast and evening dinner for the price of 3, Sunday to Friday.* 30 September to 30 April, excluding Christmas, New Year and Easter.

Cornwall 27

PENKERRIS
Penwinnick Road, St Agnes
0872-55 2262

An enchanting Edwardian country residence on the outskirts of a village. AA, RAC. Les Routiers recommended. Penkerris has fields on one side, yet pubs and shops 100 yards away on the other. There is an attractive diningroom, lounge with colour TV, video, piano, and open log fires. Single, double, twin, and family rooms are available with TV, radio, hot and cold, shaver point, tea making facilities. Delicious meals and traditional roasts served with fresh vegetables, and home made fruit tarts. Beaches, walking, swimming, surfing, gliding, magnificent cliff walks nearby.

£ *£10 per night for bed and breakfast; £17 with dinner.*
 All year.

THE GLEN HOTEL
Quay Road, St Agnes TR5 0QS
087-255 2590

A small licensed family run hotel set in half-an-acre of gardens with a view of the sea. The Coastal Path is only a few minutes' walk away. Guests at the Glen will be offered plenty of good home cooking in a relaxed and friendly atmosphere. A log fire burns in the television lounge on chillier evenings. St Agnes is central for many of the Cornish tourist attractions, while day trips to Dartmoor can be arranged at a nominal extra charge for guests without transport and staying for three days.

£ *£30 per person for two night break with dinner, bed and breakfast; £44 for three nights. £5 supplement for en suite room. 5 September to April.*

TREVAUNANCE POINT HOTEL
Trevaunance Cove, St Agnes TR5 0RZ
087-255 3235

A 17th century clifftop hotel built of granite, local stone and slate, and timbers taken from wrecked ships. A large garden, very little traffic, and the coastal footpath passing through the garden make this an ideal retreat for those seeking a relaxing break. Michelin Guide. Local seafood is a speciality on the menus, and guests can choose table d'hôte or à la carte. Bedrooms are tastefully decorated and comfortable, while the public rooms provide a cool oasis in summer and a warm and welcoming haven in winter.

£ *From £41.00 per day for break for two or three weekdays dinner, bed and breakfast. November to April.*

DALSWINTON COUNTRY HOUSE HOTEL
St Mawgan, Near Newquay TR8 4EZ
0637 860385

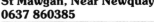

An old Cornish house of immense character standing in secluded grounds overlooking the beautiful valley of Lanherne with views to the sea. Ideally situated between Newquay and Padstow, reputed to be the finest coastline in Europe, with superb beaches and coastal walks within two miles. Under the new ownership of Geoff and Eilleen Read, the hotel has been completely refurbished and offers superb food in a friendly, comfortable atmosphere. All rooms en suite, with TVs, tea/coffee making facilities and central heating. Log fires in bar and lounge. Heated swimming pool. Open all year. AA**.

£ *Bargain Breaks 3-5 days dinner, bed and breakfast from £61.50. Open for Christmas and New Year.*

BOSSINEY HOUSE HOTEL
Tintagel PL34 0AX
0840 770240

Perched on the cliffs about half a mile from Tintagel and overlooking one of the finest stretches of coastline in Britain is the Bossiney House Hotel, offering friendly and comfortable accommodation and personal attention. AA**, RAC**. The 17 en suite bedrooms are tastefully appointed, and all enjoy sea or country views. There is a residents' bar and two lounges in which a pre or after dinner drink can be enjoyed. The hotel has fine facilities, including a heated indoor pool, sauna and solarium, outdoor activities nearby.

£ *From £55 per person for Friday and Saturday dinner, bed and breakfast. Extra nights pro rata.* ▣ *30 April to 21 July; 2 September to 31 October.*

WILLAPARK MANOR HOTEL
Bossiney, Tintagel PL34 0BA
0840 770782

Willapark Manor is a lovely character house in a beautiful setting amidst 14 acre grounds, overlooking Bossiney Bay. Surrounded by woodland, it is secluded and has direct access to the coastal path and beach. It is a family run hotel with a friendly and informal atmosphere, excellent cuisine and a well stocked cocktail bar. Beautifully appointed bedrooms, all en suite and with colour TV and tea/coffee making facilities. Some four posters. A warm welcome and a memorable holiday assured.

£ *Dinner, bed and breakfast from £172 weekly.*

LANDS VUE COUNTRY HOUSE
Lands Vue, Three Burrows TR4 8JA
0872 560242

Lands Vue is a country home set amidst two acres of peaceful gardens, with outdoor swimming pool and lots of space for croquet and other games, or just relaxing. Four lovely bedrooms with washbasins and tea-making facilities; annexe cottage room with en suite shower and WC. AA Recommended QQQ. The large dining room offers outstanding views and a friendly atmosphere in which to enjoy delicious home-made food. You are welcome to bring your own wine. Cosy lounge with log fires and TV. Ideally situated just one mile off A30; sea 3 miles, Truro 4; within easy reach of all Cornwall's beauty spots. Closed Christmas and New Year.

£ *Bed and breakfast £12 (October to May), £14 (June to September). Dinner £7. Reductions for 3 or more nights.*

TREGURRIAN HOTEL
Watergate Bay, Near Newquay
0637 860280

Standing 100 yards from Watergate Bay's glorious sandy beach and spectacular Atlantic coastline is this AA** hotel. All 27 rooms have radio and baby listening, tea makers, and most are en suite; colour TV available. The Hotel has a heated pool with sun patio, games room, sauna, jacuzzi and solarium. There is an excellent choice of food with a good wine list. Licensed bar. Tregurrian is family run, and children are welcome at reduced rates. Centrally placed for touring all parts of Cornwall.

£ *£110-£200 inc. for dinner, bed and breakfast.*
▣ *Autumn and Spring.*

Cumbria

BRACKEN FELL
Outgate, Ambleside LA22 0NH
09666 289

Bracken Fell

Bracken Fell is situated in beautiful open countryside between Ambleside and Hawkshead in the picturesque hamlet of Outgate. Ideally positioned for exploring the Lake District and within easy reach of Coniston, Windermere, Ambleside, Grasmere and Keswick. All major outdoor activities are catered for nearby, including windsurfing, sailing, fishing, pony trekking etc. All six bedrooms have washbasins, complimentary tea/coffee and outstanding views, and four have en suite facilities. There is central heating throughout, a comfortable lounge and dining room, together with ample private parking and two acres of gardens. Fire Certificate. Open all year.

£ **£28 per person for two nights bed and breakfast.**
October to May, excluding Christmas and New Year.

Kirkstone Foot Country House Hotel

Kirkstone Pass Road, Ambleside LA22 9EH
Telephone 05394 32232

Imagine a gracious and elegant 17th century manor house set in two acres of quiet and secluded gardens in the heart of the Lake District. Kirkstone Foot is just such a place. As a family-run hotel for many years, we are delighted to have earned the reputation for providing a warm welcome, caring and courteous service, excellent Egon Ronay-rated English cooking and an extensive wine cellar. Most of our guests return again and again.
All of the 15 luxurious bedrooms, studio apartments and cottages are spacious, comfortable and enjoy full private facilities. Pets are welcome in the apartments. Optional baby listening service. Special interest breaks include wine weekends and mid-week breaks. Open Christmas and New Year.

**Contact Simon & Jane Bateman & family for further details.
BTA Commended. ETB ♛♛♛♛.**

THE *Derwentwater Hotel*

AA RAC ★★★

Situated in 16 acres of delightful mature gardens on the shores of Lake Derwentwater, the Hotel accommodates its guests in 83 bedrooms, en suite, many with lake view, colour TV, radio, trouser press, hair dryer, telephone and tea/coffee making facilities are included.

Single rooms and a Four Poster Suite complete the choice available. An excellent menu is offered in the Deers Leap Restaurant and guests can relax in either of the 2 lounges or our superb conservatory. Although the Hotel is centrally heated throughout, log fires bring cheer to colder days.

For leisure hours there is a putting green and private fishing available. A children's play area and baby listening complement family visitors.

Open all year round, special event weekends.
Romantic interludes in four-poster suites.
Value for money short breaks and activity holidays available.

Telephone our helpful receptionist for colour brochure and tariff.

Derwentwater

Portinscale, KESWICK, Cumbria, England CA12 5RE
Telephone: (07687) 72538
Fax: (07687) 71002

Cumbria 31

KIRKSTONE FOOT COUNTRY HOUSE HOTEL
Kirkstone Pass Road, Ambleside LA22 9EH
053-94 32232

Kirkstone Foot is a gracious and elegant seventeenth century manor house, set in two acres of secluded grounds in the heart of the Lake District. This family-run hotel has a wide reputation for providing caring and courteous service, excellent English cooking, and an extensive wine cellar. All 15 luxurious bedrooms, studio apartments and cottages are spacious and comfortable, with full private facilities. Pets are welcome in the apartments. Special interest breaks include wine weekends and mid-week breaks.

£ **£35-£47.50 per person per night, dinner, bed and breakfast. Wine tasting weekends November-February: minimum two night stay — from £110 including dinner, bed, breakfast and all wines.**

LANGDALE HOTEL AND COUNTRY CLUB
Great Langdale, Near Ambleside LA22 9JD
09667 302

Charming Lake District hotel in 35 acres of beautifully landscaped grounds surrounded by breathtaking scenery. Wide choice of outdoor activities – walking, horse riding, sailing, tennis and fishing. 65 bedrooms, all with luxury bathroom, satellite TV, radio and direct-dial telephone. The Country Club offers indoor swimming pool, squash, gymnasium, steam room, solaria and hydro spa. Excellent food and friendly, attentive staff. Civic Trust Award, BTA Award, AA*** RAC****, Egon Ronay Recommended.

£ **From £118 for two people sharing double room per night (dinner, bed and breakfast). Minimum 2 nights.**
Until April 1991.

NANNY BROW COUNTRY HOUSE HOTEL   Commended
Ambleside LA22 9NF
05394 32036

"An OASIS of ELEGANCE" is how most guides describe the Nanny Brow Hotel, set in some 5 acres of formal gardens and woodland overlooking the spectacular Langdale valley. Most bedrooms have stunning views, all en suite with colour television, FREE satellite channels, tea/coffee making, minibars and direct-dial telephones. 7 suites in our garden wing with either a terrace or balcony; the Hotel suite has a FOUR-POSTER BED; all have a sitting area. Our weekend breaks can include a Sunday night for only 50% of our normal rates. BTA 4 Crowns Commended, Egon Ronay, Arthur Eperon, Les Routiers, Ashley Courtenay Recommended.

£ **From £89 per person for Friday and Saturday dinner, bed and breakfast and Sunday lunch. October to May.**

MILBURN GRANGE   Commended
Appleby-in-Westmorland CA16 6DR
07683 61867

Four quality cottages, all equipped to highest standards, set in 2 acres in a tiny hamlet at the foot of the Pennines. All have colour TV and microwaves; all except smallest have washing machines and largest have dishwashers. Linen inc., also cots and high chairs. Children's play area; babysitting available. This is an excellent walking/touring base — Ullswater 11 miles, Appleby 5. Shop, Post Office and garage close by, public house within walking distance. Two other properties available in nearby villages. Open all year. For details please send SAE to Mrs M.J. Burke.

£ **3 day bargain break for couples £65 including linen and central heating. November-May except Christmas week.**

HOWE FOOT HOLIDAY FLATS
Bowness-on-Windermere
09662 2792

Howe Foot Holiday Flats offer an excellent opportunity to have a comfortable and inexpensive carefree holiday. Open all year round, the flats are conveniently, yet privately, situated just a few minutes' walk from buses, shops and Lake Windermere. All beds have spring interior mattresses and bed linen is provided; cots and bedding available at no extra cost. Laundry room. Electricity by slot meter. Supplies of eggs and milk delivered daily and may be ordered in advance. Private parking. For details contact Mrs M. Thexton, Quarry Lodge, Oakthwaite Road, Windermere LA23 2BD. ETB Approved.
£ *Long weekends available November-March (full weeks only Christmas and New Year), also mid-week bookings. From £45.*

THE BLACKSMITH'S ARMS
Talkin Village, Brampton CA8 1LE
06977 3452

[TA]

The Blacksmith's Arms offer all the hospitality and comforts of a traditional country inn. Enjoy tasty meals served in the bar lounges or linger over dinner in the well-appointed restaurant. There are five lovely bedrooms, all en suite and offering every comfort. Peacefully situated in the beautiful village of Talkin, the Inn is convenient for the Borders, Hadrian's Wall and the Lake District. Good golf course, pony trekking, walking and other country pursuits nearby. FHG Best Bed and Breakfast Diploma Winners 1989. Personally managed by the proprietors Pat and Tom Bagshaw.

£ *On application.* Spring and autumn.

CRAIGBURN FARM
Catlowdy, Penton, Carlisle CA6 5QP
0228-77 214

Commended [TA]

Enjoy the delights of beautiful Cumbrian countryside and life on our 250-acre working farm. Ideal for a "get away from it all" holiday. Relax in the peace and quiet of the farmhouse, with delicious farmhouse cooking, comfort and a friendly atmosphere guaranteed. Ideal for travel to/from Scotland. AA Listed. All bedrooms have central heating, are en suite and have tea-making facilities. Four-poster bed available. Residential drinks licence; games room. Short Breaks discounts and 10% discount on weekly bookings. Certificate of Merit "Great British Breakfast" 1989, Finalist in Farm and Food Year National Cookery Competition.
£ *Bed and breakfast from £16-£18; dinner, bed and breakfast from £25-£27. All year.*

NEW PALLYARDS
Hethersgill, Carlisle CA6 6HZ
0228 77308

Commended [TA]

We welcome you to our beef/sheep farm, nine miles north of Junction 44 on M6, which has been filmed for BBC TV. An ideal base for the Lakes, Scottish Borders and Hadrian's Wall. Local salmon and sea trout fishing. Good home cooking. Two family rooms and two double, all en suite; one single and one twin room with H&C. AA, HWFH, FHB, Gold Award. Also self-catering accommodation in a comfortable, well appointed bungalow with 3/4 bedrooms, two lovely cottages on a working farm (all 4 Keys). Video available for small refundable deposit.
£ *£45 per person for 2 nights dinner, bed and breakfast. Extra nights pro rata. Self-catering — 2 nights £56, 3 nights £65.*

Cumbria 33

STRING OF HORSES INN
Faugh, Carlisle CA4 7EG
0228 70297/70509

A picturesque 17th century inn which enjoys the luxuries of a five star hotel. All the bedrooms are en suite, and some have four poster beds and double baths. Guests may relax with a drink in the lounge or cocktail bar before going on to enjoy their meal in the restaurant. The hotel has a sauna, solarium, whirlpool spa, and outdoor heated pool. Golf and fishing nearby. The String of Horses is ideal for touring, being equidistant from the Northern Lakes, the Borders, the Solway Coast, and the Roman Wall. RAC***, AA*** and Bedroom Award.
£ *From £50 per person for two nights bed and breakfast. Other meals optional.* ☐ *October to April.*

THE CUMBRIAN HOTEL
Court Square, Carlisle CA1 1QY
0228 31951 Fax: 0228 47799

The Cumbrian Hotel is an elegant Victorian building fronting the historic, cobbled Court Square. The generously proportioned and elegantly styled rooms are furnished with comfort as the main consideration, and bedrooms are complete with private bathroom, satellite TV, radio, telephone and tea/coffee facilities. Suites and executive rooms are also available. The restaurant recalls the era when Queen Victoria halted at the hotel for lunch en route to Balmoral Castle. There is a superb à la carte menu, and snacks are available in the Cumbrian Kitchen coffee shop. Ideally placed for touring the Lake District, all parts within easy reach.
£ *Breakaway Weekends: Celebration, Horse-racing, Heritage, Steam Railway.* ☐ *Details available on request.*

THE QUEEN'S ARMS INN AND MOTEL
Warwick-on-Eden, Carlisle CA4 8PA
0228 60699

Situated four miles east of Carlisle and only a few minutes' drive from the M6, the Queen's Arms is an ideal base for exploring Hadrian's Wall, the Scottish Borders, the Lake District and the rolling Cumbrian fells. All bedrooms are en suite, with television and tea/coffee making facilities. The à la carte restaurant offers delicious meals, complemented by a carefully selected wine list; an extensive bar snack menu is also available. There is a modern adventure playground where children can safely play. Dogs welcome and allowed in bedrooms by arrangement.
£ *2 or 3 night weekend breaks available — terms on application.*

BESSIESTOWN FARM
Catlowdy, Penton, Carlisle CA6 5QP
0228 77 219

Visitors to Bessiestown are assured of a warm friendly welcome and a relaxed atmosphere on this small beef and sheep rearing farm, ideally situated for touring and as a stopover to/from Scotland and Northern Ireland. All bedrooms are en suite, with tea/coffee facilities, and there is a comfortable lounge bar and television lounge. AA Award Winner, RAC Acclaimed. Indoor heated swimming pool. Delicious home cooking. Residential licence. Restricted smoking area. Three self-catering cottages also available, with the option of an evening meal.
£ *From £35 per person for 2 nights bed and breakfast (based on 2 sharing double room). Dinner optional.* ☐ *All year.*

34 Cumbria

WILSON ARMS
Torver, Near Coniston LA21 8BB
05394 41237

Friendly guest house and inn situated in the beautiful Lake District within easy reach of Coniston Water and the central Lakes. Ideal walking area with miles of unspoilt countryside; fishing and riding also available in the area. The comfortable bedrooms (some en suite) have TV and tea/coffee making facilities. The Wilson Arms makes a perfect base at any time of year, with the welcome prospect of a delicious home-cooked meal and a cosy log fire at the end of the day. Les Routiers recommended.

£ *3 nights' bed and breakfast for the price of 2 nights.*
November, December, January (except Christmas and New Year).

GREEN VIEW LODGES
Green View, Welton, Near Dalston CA5 7ES
06996 230

Commended
♛♛♛♛/♛♛♛♛

Three luxury Scandinavian pine lodges peacefully situated in own grounds in picturesque hamlet on fringe of Lake District National Park. These WTB Grade 5 Award lodges sleep from 4 to 6 persons in 2/3 bedrooms and all are luxuriously equipped with colour TV, automatic washing machine, heaters and microwave. Each property has shower/bath and WC. The lodges are open all year and are ideal for an off-season break. Cumbria and Lakeland Self Catering Association. SAE, please, for details of brochure and video.

£ *Special winter mid-week breaks — 4 nights for the price of 3 — arriving Monday and leaving Friday — from £90 per couple inclusive of heating, linen and cancellation insurance.*

HARE AND HOUNDS INN
Bowland Bridge, Grange-over-Sands
044-88 333

With a tranquil situation in the beautiful Winster valley and yet convenient for Windermere, the Hare and Hounds is a delightful, residential hostelry with a warm welcome for all. The lounge bar with its oak beams, stone walls and log fires, has a typical Lakeland atmosphere. There is a beer garden and, isolated by the rolling Cartmel Fells, the inn, which dates from 1600, is conveniently placed for numerous beauty spots and places of historic interest. There are 16 bedrooms, most en suite, and all with telephone; also a lounge. Access and Visa welcome.

£ *From £56 per person for 2 nights dinner, bed and breakfast. Extra nights pro rata.* *All year.*

BORWICK LODGE
Outgate, Hawkshead, Ambleside LA22 0PU
096-66 332

A rather special 17th century country house with magnificent panoramic views of the lakes and mountains, quietly secluded in 3 acres of beautiful landscaped gardens. Close to Hawkshead village with its good choice of restaurants and inns. Tastefully furnished en suite bedrooms have colour TV, tea/coffee facilities and outstanding views. "Special Occasion" four-poster room. Linda and Alan Bleasdale aim to make you feel welcome and relaxed at this "haven of peace and tranquillity". NON-SMOKING. Open all year. Self-catering cottage also available.

£ *Bed and breakfast from £15.*

Cumbria 35

OVERWATER HALL
Ireby, Carlisle CA5 1HH
059-681 566

Set amongst 18 acres of mature woodlands and gardens, Overwater Hall is peacefully secluded, yet within minutes of the popular centres of the Lake District. All the comfortable, en suite bedrooms have colour TV, radio, hairdryers and tea/coffee making facilities. There is a spacious drawing room, lounge, cocktail bar, snooker room and sun terrace. The pleasant dining room is renowned for its attractive and varied menu, good service and well-stocked wine cellar. The Hall is family-run and retains an informal country house atmosphere, while offering comfort, beauty and peaceful surroundings. AA/RAC**.

£ *Any two days dinner, bed and breakfast £70 per person (Friday and Saturday), £66 midweek.*
☐ *October 1990 – June 1991.*

COTTAGE IN THE WOOD
Whinlatter Pass, Keswick CA12 5TW
059-682 409

Commended

Once a 17th century coaching inn the Cottage in the Wood is now a small, comfortable hotel set beautifully and remotely on Whinlatter Pass in the heart of Thornthwaite Forest and enjoying superb views to Skiddaw. Owners Sandra and Barrie Littlefair look forward to welcoming all their guests. The Cottage in the Wood enjoys a fine reputation for excellent and thoughtfully prepared traditional food. All bedrooms have hot drink facilities and central heating, and most have en suite facilities.

£ *£58, £78, £104 per person for two, three and four nights respectively for dinner, bed and breakfast with en suite room.* ☐ *April to July, November.*

GRETA VIEW HOUSE
2 Greta Street, Keswick CA12 4HS
07687 73102

A picturesque early 19th century licensed private hotel just 3 minutes' walk into Keswick or to Leisure Pool. Lovely views over river to Skiddaw (over 3000ft). In the beautiful heart of Northern Lakeland, within easy reach of most major peaks, lakes and all types of outdoor pursuits, offering spacious, warm and comfortable accommodation all year round in friendly, relaxed surroundings. RAC Listed. Whether for fun-filled, activity-packed family holidays, or quiet, intimate breaks with en suite shower or bathroom, Greta View caters for all. Full central heating, colour TV and tea/coffee facilities in all rooms.

£ *From £17.50 per person per night for bed and breakfast. Evening Meal optional. Reduced rates for children sharing.*
☐ *Available all year, no supplementary charges.*

LATRIGG LODGE HOTEL
Lake Road, Keswick CA12 5DQ
07687 73545

Latrigg Lodge is a small luxury hotel situated close to the town centre and the Lake. Ashley Courtenay. Les Routiers. AA. All seven double bedrooms are well appointed, with colour television, hairdryer, and tea and coffee making facilities. Two rooms also have four poster beds. Latrigg Lodge has a top international chef providing superb table d'hôte and à la carte cuisine. The hotel is ideally placed for touring in this most lovely corner of England.

£ *£60 per person for a two night break of bed, breakfast and table d'hôte dinner, or £12 allowance towards à la carte. Three and four night breaks also available.* ☐ *All year except Bank Holidays.*

LYZZICK HALL HOTEL
Underskiddaw, Keswick CA12 4PY
076-87 72277

Enchanting Victorian Manor house in three acre grounds with breathtaking panoramic mountain views. AA**, RAC**. Superb walking area. Also tremendous range of outdoor pursuits. Full licence, central heating throughout, log fires. Friendly and informal atmosphere. Excellent local reputation for fine food. Twenty bedrooms, all en suite, all with TV (with video channel), radio, telephone and tea/coffee making facilities. Outdoor swimming pool.
[£] *£60 per person for minimum two nights dinner, bed and breakfast with en suite facilities. Extra nights pro rata.* ☼ *November to end of April, excluding Christmas and Easter.*

THE DERWENTWATER HOTEL
Portinscale, Keswick CA12 5RE
07687 72538

Situated in 16 acres of delightful mature grounds on the shore of Lake Derwentwater, the hotel accommodates guests in 83 en suite bedrooms. All have colour TV, radio, telephone, tea/coffee facilities, trouser press and hair dryer. An excellent menu is offered in the Deer's Leap Restaurant, and guests can relax in either of the two lounges or conservatory. The hotel is centrally heated throughout, with log fires for colder days. Putting green and private fishing available; also children's play area and baby listening. AA and RAC***.
[£] ☼ *Open all year round for special event weekends e.g. Short Break and Activity Holidays. Telephone for colour brochure and tariff.*

WHOOP HALL INN
Burrow-with-Burrow, Kirkby Lonsdale LA6 2HP
05242 71284

Commended

This delightful inn is extremely well-placed for touring both Lakes and Dales, and is only 6 miles from the M6 (Junction 36). All bedrooms are in country cottage style, and are en suite, with direct-dial telephone, colour TV and beverage making facilities. A charming four-poster room, complete with jacuzzi is also available. AA/RAC**, Les Routiers. Booking in advance is recommended at the deservedly popular Gallery Restaurant, and a selection of traditional English and pasta dishes are featured at the Buttery.
[£] *Any 2 days dinner, bed and full English breakfast £65 per person. Additional days £32.50 per person.* ☼ *1991 (excluding Christmas and Bank Holidays).*

TEMPLE SOWERBY HOUSE HOTEL
Temple Sowerby, Near Penrith CA10 1RZ
076-83 61578

Formerly the principal house of the village, parts of this lovely hotel dates back to 1504, with Georgian additions. Rooms are spacious and beautifully furnished, while public rooms are elegant yet comfortable. In winter guests may relax before the glowing fires, while drinks may be taken in the Conservatory or on the terrace in spring and summer, when the walled garden and Lakeland hills are at their prettiest. Conveniently situated in the lovely Eden Valley for both Lakes and Dales. Resident Proprietor Rosemary Edwards.
[£] *£75 per person for two nights dinner, bed and breakfast. £85 for four poster room with champagne on arrival.* ☼ *All year except Bank Holidays and Appleby Horse Fair.*

Cumbria 37

GOLF HOTEL
Criffel Street, Silloth-on-Solway CA5 4AB
06973 31438 Fax: 06973 32582

The Golf Hotel is a well-appointed, licensed hotel, conveniently situated overlooking the Solway Firth and near the Lake District, Roman Wall and Scottish Borders. Silloth is ideal for enjoying a wide range of activities, including golf, climbing, sailing, fishing and riding. The comfortably furnished rooms, all en suite, have tea/coffee facilities, colour TV, radio and direct-dial telephone. A wide choice of excellent food is served in the restaurant, complemented by a comprehensive wine list. Silloth enjoys good road links with the M6 motorway and is only a short drive from Carlisle. AA**, RAC***, Ashley Courtenay Recommended.

[£] *Details of Getaway Breaks available on request.*

WHITEWATER HOTEL
The Lakeland Village, Newby Bridge, Ulverston LA12 8PX
05395 31133

This impressive building, originally a mill, has been transformed into a luxury hotel of the highest standards. All bedrooms are en suite with satellite TV, direct-dial telephone, tea/coffee facilities and mini-bar. In the hotel restaurant which overlooks the river, guests may enjoy delicious meals from the extensive menu. During their stay guests have free use of the adjacent Leisure Club, with heated indoor swimming pool, whirlpool, and exercise studio. Nearby is a sporting estate where riding, fishing, clay shooting, deer stalking, archery and windsurfing can all be enjoyed.

[£] *Special Mini-breaks, minimum 2 nights stay, from £53.00 per person per night for dinner, bed and breakfast.*

CROWN HOTEL
Station Road, Wetheral CA4 8ES
0228 61888

This lovely Grade II Listed hotel is located in the picture-postcard village of Wetheral. All 49 bedrooms have en suite bathroom, satellite colour TV, tea/coffee facilities, direct-dial telephone etc. The hotel's Leisure Club offers some of the finest facilities in the area — swimming pool, spa pool, sauna, solarium, gymnasium, squash courts and snooker tables, all available for guests' use. You can enjoy a wide selection of traditional and speciality dishes in the relaxing surroundings of the Conservatory Restaurant, or a pint of award-winning ale in Walton's Bar.

[£] *Minimum of 2 nights dinner, bed and breakfast £45 per person per night sharing room. Includes £14 dinner allowance and full use of leisure facilities.*

HAWKSMOOR GUEST HOUSE
Lake Road, Windermere LA23 2EQ
096-62 2110

A friendly, family run guest house surrounded by extensive gardens and private woodlands, Hawksmoor offers peace and quiet for a relaxing short break holiday. All 10 bedrooms are comfortably furnished, with en suite facilities, colour TV, tea/coffee making facilities, and each enjoys lovely garden or woodland views. A full English breakfast will set you up for a day seeing the delights of Lakeland. Hawksmoor's cosy lounge is the ideal setting for an aperitif before your evening meal. AA, RAC Highly Acclaimed.

[£] *£50 for two nights dinner, bed and breakfast. £74 for three nights. Some discounts for stays including a Sunday.* ☐ *November to April.*

38 *Cumbria*

HOLBECK GHYLL COUNTRY HOUSE HOTEL
Holbeck Lane, Windermere LA23 1LU
05394 32375

Between Ambleside and Windermere, set back half a mile from the main road, Holbeck Ghyll offers the perfect setting for a peaceful, relaxing break. In its own immaculate grounds overlooking Lake Windermere, the hotel features modern facilities within the 19th century country house, which was once owned by Lord Lonsdale. Five-course dinners with ample choice throughout and prepared with the freshest produce are served in the oak-panelled restaurant. RAC and AA**. Other amenities include a snooker room and putting green.
£ *From £40 per person per night for 5-course dinner, en suite room and English breakfast (minimum 2 nights).* ⊟ *February to May; November and December.*

LINDETH HOWE COUNTRY HOUSE HOTEL
Windermere LA23 3JF
096-62 5759

Once the home of Beatrix Potter, this hotel stands in six acres overlooking Lake Windermere. Many of the 13 bedrooms enjoy splendid views across the Lake, and all have colour TV, hot drinks making facilities, radio, telephone, and central heating. Some four-posters. Cosy lounge, inglenook fireplace and log fire. The intimate atmosphere is maintained in the candlelit restaurant. Sauna, solarium, pool table for guests' use. Outdoor leisure facilities within reach. Ashley Courtenay and Les Routiers recommended.
£ *From £41.50 for dinner, bed and breakfast; prices dependent upon season.* ⊟ *November to April excluding Christmas and Easter; May to October.*

ROCKSIDE
Ambleside Road, Windermere LA23 1AQ
09662 5343

Rockside is built of traditional Lakeland stone and slate, and is full of character yet with all modern amenities. RAC Acclaimed. Two minutes' walk from town centre and ideal for touring the whole of the Lake District. Help given to plan routes and walks. Single, twin, double and family rooms available, all with colour TV, telephone, clock/radio and central heating. Most have en suite bathroom, tea/coffee facilities and hairdryer. Choice of breakfast. Large car park. Open all year as every season in the Lake District has its own magic.
£ *Bed and breakfast from £13.50 to £20.50 per person, half price for children sharing. Reductions for longer stays.* ⊟ *All year.*

PUBLISHER'S NOTE

While every effort is made to ensure accuracy, we regret that FHG Publications cannot accept responsibility for errors, omissions or misrepresentation in our entries or any consequences thereof. Prices in particular should be checked because we go to press early. We will follow up complaints but cannot act as arbiters or agents for either party.

SOUTH VIEW HOTEL
Cross Street, Windermere LA23 1AE
09662 2951

Our 140-year-old house is situated in a quiet, sunny position, yet central for shops and transport. Golf, walking, fishing, boating and stately homes are all close at hand. Be in the swim, wet or fine. Relax in our spa pool after a hard day's sightseeing. You can be sure of a warm welcome at any time. Why not take it easy for a few days?

£ *2 days bed and breakfast £38; 2 days bed, breakfast and 5-course dinner £56.* ☐ *1.11.90 to 23.12.90 and 2.1.91 to 31.3.91.*

ST. JOHN'S LODGE
Lake Road, Windermere LA23 2EQ
096-62 3078

A private hotel situated midway between Windermere and the Lake. Close to all amenities. AA, RAC Highly Acclaimed, Les Routiers, Ashley Courtenay. The 14 bedrooms have en suite facilities and are comfortably furnished, with colour TV and tea/coffee making facilities. Centrally heated throughout. There is a comfortable lounge for residents, and a friendly bar, where you are invited to take an aperitif, before enjoying a four-course dinner which has been personally prepared by the chef/proprietor.
£ *£47 for 2 nights dinner, bed and breakfast; £68 for 3 nights. Reduced rates for bed and breakfast for 4 night stays.* ☐ *November to April inclusive, excluding Christmas and Easter.*

Other specialised
FHG PUBLICATIONS

* Recommended COUNTRY HOTELS OF BRITAIN   £2.99

* Recommended WAYSIDE INNS OF BRITAIN   £2.99

* PETS WELCOME!   £2.50

* BED AND BREAKFAST IN BRITAIN   £1.99

Published annually. Please add 50p postage (U.K. only) when ordering from the publishers:

**FHG PUBLICATIONS LTD
Abbey Mill Business Centre, Seedhill,
Paisley, Renfrewshire PA1 1JN**

Derbyshire

THE DOG AND PARTRIDGE COUNTRY INN
Swinscoe, Ashbourne DE6 2HS
0335 43183

Mary and Martin Stelfox welcome you to a family-run 17th century inn and motel set in five acres, 5 miles from Alton Towers and close to Dovedale and Ashbourne. We specialise in family breaks, and special diets and vegetarians are catered for. All rooms have private bathrooms, colour TV, direct-dial telephone, tea making facilities and baby listening service. Ideal for touring Stoke Potteries, Derbyshire Dales and Staffordshire moorlands. Restaurant open all day, non-residents welcome.

£ *Any 2 nights dinner, bed and breakfast midweek £56, weekend £60 per person.*

RIVERSIDE COUNTRY HOUSE HOTEL
Ashford-in-the-Water, Bakewell
0629 814275

A luxurious country house hotel set in one acre of mature garden with river frontage, in the Peak District National Park. Michelin. Lounges and restaurant are furnished with antiques, and are warmed by log fires. Bedrooms — some with four posters — are all en suite, and have direct dial telephones, tea and coffee making facilities, TV, and radio. A daily changing menu is served in the renowned gourmet restaurant, with fresh foods in season. Ideally situated for visiting Chatsworth, Haddon, and Hardwick Halls. Riverside is a haven in which to just relax.

£ *£126.50 for two nights dinner, bed and breakfast. Extra nights pro rata. All year except Christmas, when special breaks are arranged.*

THE MANOR HOTEL AND RESTAURANT
High Street, Dronfield S18 6PY
0246 413971

 [TA]

The Manor Hotel is a delightful 16th and 18th century listed building which has been tastefully converted into an attractive hotel and licensed restaurant. AA and RAC**. It is situated in the centre of Old Dronfield, which lies at the edge of the Peak District National Park. The en suite bedrooms are centrally heated, and have colour TV and tea/coffee facilities. The restaurant is renowned for excellent cuisine and fine wines, and offers a friendly atmosphere in a picturesque setting.

£ *From £33.50 single, £42.75 double for bed and full English breakfast.*

Derbyshire 41

THE CHARLES COTTON HOTEL
Hartington, Near Buxton SK17 0AL
0298 84229

The Charles Cotton is a small, comfortable hotel with a starred rating for the AA and RAC. The hotel lies in the heart of the Derbyshire Dales, pleasantly situated in the village square of Hartington, with nearby shops catering for all needs. It is renowned throughout the area for its hospitality and good home cooking. Pets and children are welcome; special diets catered for. The Charles Cotton makes the perfect centre to relax and explore the area, whether walking, cycling, pony trekking or even hang gliding.

£ *Special rates for mini-breaks and weekly rates. Please phone for details.*

THE TEMPLE HOTEL AND RESTAURANT
Matlock Bath DE4 3PG
0629 583911

The Hotel, AA and RAC Approved, is situated on the hills, halfway up to the Heights of Abraham, and enjoys commanding views over the valley — almost like Austria. Visited by Princess Victoria at the age of 13, it is ideally situated within a few miles of the Peaks and stately homes and half an hour from Alton Towers. All 14 bedrooms are en suite, with colour television and telephone. Austrian/French cuisine is served in the Panorama Restaurant; there is also a Carvery. Proprietors Mr and Mrs Essl provide Austrian style hospitality.

£ *Terms on application.* ⌂ *October to May, excluding Bank Holiday weekends.*

PARK HALL HOTEL
Spinkhill, Sheffield S31 9YD
0246 434897

Sixteenth century manor house hotel set in eight and a half acres of landscaped grounds, one mile from Junction 30 of M1. Within driving distance of Peak District National Park; golf within one mile, sports centre 5 miles. All bedrooms are en suite, with colour television, tea/coffee making facilities and direct-dial telephones. RAC***. Other amenities include residents' lounge, and licensed bar. The Uplands Manor restaurant serves table d'hôte and à la carte dinners.

£ *Bed, full English breakfast and dinner £71.50 per person (2 nights); £93.50 (3 nights). Additional nights pro rata.* ⌂ *All year, except Easter, Christmas, New Year, and last weekend in May.*

EXPLANATION OF SYMBOLS

TA	Travel Agency Commission
♛	Number of Crowns
⚲	Number of Keys
🐕	Pets Welcome
🎠	Reductions for Children
♿	Suitable for Disabled
🎄	Christmas Breaks

Devon

BEACH & BRACKEN HOLIDAYS
Bratton Fleming, Barnstaple EX31 4TJ
0598 710702

Beach and Bracken Holidays is a booking service for village, farmhouse and self-catering accommodation in the spectacular countryside between Exmoor and the sea. Recommended farm accommodation is comfortable, and has excellent food, and there is a full range of self-catering properties from which guests can choose. Advice is given to guests on how best to make the most of their short break holidays in this lovely corner of England.

£ *Bed and breakfast from £12; self-catering from £90 for winter weekend breaks.* All year; self-catering weekend breaks available in winter months.

Heron House Hotel
Thurlestone Sands · Salcombe · South Devon

* Ashley Courtenay recommended
* At the edge of the sea
* Surrounded by unspoilt countryside
* Set in idyllic surroundings
* Probably the finest location to be found
* 18 beautifully appointed bedrooms
* All with stunning coastal and rural views
* All ensuite, colour TVs and teamaking

* Direct dial telephones in all rooms
* Large outdoor swim pool – heated May to September
* First class cuisine, supervised by Proprietor
* Specialising in Devon produce
* Comfortable bar lounge, separate quiet lounge
* OFF SEASON BREAKS
* Personal service by the Rowland family

Telephone for reservations (Mrs Rowland): 0548 561308

Woolacombe Bay Hotel
Woolacombe   EX34 7BN   Telephone (0271) 870388

An elegant, gracious ★★★ Hotel set in 6 acres of grounds running down to Woolacombe's 3 miles of golden sands. Built in the days of gracious living, the hotel exudes a feeling of luxury and traditional style, coupled with a lively sporting complex with FREE UNLIMITED use of squash, tennis, 2 swimming pools, fitness room, spa bath, sauna, solarium, aerobic and aquarobic classes, billiards, children's organiser and lots more.

All rooms with bath, toilet, shower, hairdryer, TV, radio, in-house video, satellite TV, direct dial telephone, tea making facilities and baby listening.

Relaxation is easy, but for the person with boundless energy the Woolacombe Bay Hotel has a sportsman's choice of amenities and a variety of indoor pursuits available.

An elegant hotel on Devon's golden coast.

FOX AND HOUNDS
Fremington, Near Barnstaple
0271 73094

A friendly and attractive village inn on the Barnstaple to Bideford road, the Fox and Hounds offers the informal, uncomplicated pleasures enjoyed by lovers of the simple life. WCTB. Accommodation is wholesome, and the bars invite relaxation over a quiet drink or by playing darts, pool, shove ha'penny, or skittles. Conveniently placed for a number of tourist attractions, including Woolacombe and Westward Ho!, the nearby Taw Estuary, Exmoor, and the rugged appeal of Lynton and Lynmouth.

£ *£25 per night for bed and breakfast.* All year.

SANDY COVE HOTEL
Combe Martin Bay, Berrynarbor
0271 882243

Enjoy a short break holiday at this Relais Routiers recommended hotel overlooking a beautiful bay, the sea, and Exmoor. Bedrooms are equipped to a high standard, and all have private bathroom. The restaurant offers table d'hôte or an extensive à la carte choice, including Caribbean and lobster dishes. There is live entertainment, including dances and country and western cabaret. Sandy Cove's facilities include a heated outdoor pool, fitness room, sauna, whirlpool, and sunbed. Fully licensed.

£ *From £91 plus VAT for two days; if you can take an extra day it will be free.* All year, excluding high season and Bank Holidays.

WHEEL FARM COUNTRY COTTAGES
Berry Down 3, Near Combe Martin EX34 0NT
0271 882100

An oasis of tranquillity with magnificent views across Exmoor, yet near unspoilt sandy beaches. Excellent position for touring, walking or just relaxing. Cosy luxury cottages in traditional watermill and barn conversions, nestling in 8 acres of gardens and woodlands. Central heating, wood-burning stoves, dishwashers, microwaves, fridge-freezers, four-poster beds, shop and laundry. Linen and maid service inclusive. Home cooked meals provided. Caring, friendly owners. Cottages sleep 2-7 persons.
[£] *£56 for 2 persons for 3 nights; £72 for 6 persons for 3 nights. Minimum two night booking.* ☐ *29 September to 11 May.*

RIVERSFORD HOTEL
Limers Lane, Bideford EX39 2RG
0237 474239/470381

   [TA]

A country house hotel set in tranquil gardens with magnificent views over the River Torridge. AA**, RAC**; Les Routiers. Member of Inter-Hotel. There are moorings in the grounds for boats as well as fishing, badminton, and putting. Golf nearby. A la carte or table d'hôte menus are available in the restaurant, and there is a cocktail bar. Within minutes of the ancient ports of Bideford and Appledore; the golden sands of Westward Ho! and Instow, and the unique village of Clovelly. Exmoor and North Cornwall also in easy reach.
[£] *£84 per person for two nights table d'hôte dinner, bed and full English breakfast. Extra nights pro rata.* ☐ *All year.*

DEVONCOURT HOLIDAY FLATS
Berryhead Road, Brixham TQ5 9AB
08-045 3748

[TA]

The Devoncourt Holiday Flats are a modern, purpose built block of 24 flats, containing all modern conveniences. The flats offer accommodation for up to six persons, with private bathrooms and colour television. They have their own private balcony overlooking Brixham Marina and Torbay. Linen on hire if required. Boating and open air swimming pool only 200 yards away. Beautiful beach opposite. Open all year.

[£] ☐ *Full details on request.*

RICHMOND HOUSE
Manor Road, Brixham TQ5 8HA
0803 882391

 [TA]

Detached Victorian house of character with a relaxed and friendly atmosphere, quietly located yet central for shops and historic harbour, and with a licensed restaurant 100 yards away. This is an excellent base for touring the South Hams and Dartmoor, three-quarters of an hour from the M5. There are pleasant coastal walks and river boat trips, and three historic towns to browse around. The 8 spacious bedrooms have washbasins and pleasant views; en suite available. Cosy lounge, tea making facilities, extensive library and games. Credit cards accepted.
[£] *Bed and varied 4-course breakfast from £13 per person per night.* ☐ *March to October inclusive.*

Devon 45

FURZELEIGH MILL COUNTRY HOUSE HOTEL
Dart Bridge, Buckfastleigh TQ11 0JP
0364 43476

Situated in own grounds in beautiful countryside within Dartmoor National Park, this former 16th century mill is an excellent touring centre for South Devon, Dartmoor and the nearby coast. It is noted for excellent food, hospitality and comfort. Residents' lounge, cosy bar, character beamed restaurant, attractive bedrooms overlooking the countryside and with TV and tea-making. AA Listed.

£ *Bargain mid-week and weekend rates.* ☐ *Open all year.*

THE NEW INN HOTEL
Clovelly, Near Bideford EX39 5SY
02373 636

This beautiful hotel boasts a perfect blend of traditional splendour and modern amenities. Luggage is transported from the nearby car park by donkey and sledge to the lovely hotel with its dark oak timbers and white-washed stone frontage. The varied menu includes local produce and fresh fish. Situated just ten miles from Bideford, the New Inn Hotel is a relaxing hideaway for the discerning holiday-maker. There are many scenic walks nearby and, for the angler, plenty of opportunities for sea fishing.

£ *From £39 per person for two nights dinner, bed and breakfast. Extra nights pro rata.* ☐ *October to April.*

DRUPE FARM
Colaton Raleigh, Sidmouth EX10 0LE
0395 68838

Commended

This former farmhouse has been imaginatively and stylishly converted to provide a selection of very high quality self-catering cottages, located round a landscaped courtyard. Each cottage has a living/dining room with fully equipped kitchen area, bathroom and WC. The smallest have two bedrooms sleeping 4, while the largest can sleep up to 7. Bed linen, colour TV, cots, electricity and full gas central heating all included. Games room and laundry; resident warden. Situated on edge of pretty Devon village 3 miles from coast and within 5 miles of Sidmouth and Budleigh Salterton.

£ *Short Breaks always available Oct.-March and by arrangement at other times; 1991 rates for minimum stay of 2 nights from £45-£136, weekly rates from £112 to £339 (depending on season).*

COMPTON POOL FARM
Compton TQ3 1TA
0803 872241

These luxury period farmyard cottages offer a self-catering country break. Set in over 12 acres of countryside, all enjoy superb views. Linen and colour TV are provided in every cottage. AA, ETB. Facilities for guests include a fully equipped games barn, indoor pool, sauna, children's playground, tennis court, trout lake, and a laundry. Compton Pool Farm is close to Dartmoor and three miles from the sea, so riding and sailing are just two of the pursuits available nearby.

£ *From £60 for weekend breaks.*
☐ *November to March.*

EBFORD HOUSE HOTEL
Exmouth Road, Ebford EX3 0QH
0392 877658

This lovingly restored Georgian country house, set in beautiful gardens, has an excellent reputation for first-class cuisine, complemented by fine wines. Bedrooms are all en-suite, attractively furnished and well-equipped, and enjoy views over the beautiful surrounding countryside. The leisure area incorporates a sauna, solarium and jacuzzi, together with several pieces of keep-fit apparatus. The Cathedral city of Exeter is only four miles away, with the Maritime Museum, theatre and shopping centre. Dartmoor National Park is also within easy reach, and sailing, golf and horse-riding are all available nearby. AA and RAC**. Ashley Courtenay Recommended.

£ *2 nights dinner, bed and breakfast for 2 people sharing – £165.* ✇ *Available October to April excluding Bank Holidays.*

LORD HALDON HOTEL
Dunchideock, Near Exeter EX6 7YF
0392 832483

A lovely historic family run country house hotel standing in peaceful grounds with panoramic views over the Exe Valley. Relais Routiers. RAC***. All the 26 comfortably furnished bedrooms are en suite. Traditional hospitality greets guests throughout and a friendly welcome. The hotel has two relaxing bars, and good food and wine is served in the restaurant. There is ample parking for guests. The Lord Haldon is ideally placed for touring this lovely part of England with the coast, and Exmoor and Dartmoor, all within easy reach.

£ *£65 for any two days dinner, bed and breakfast.* ✇ *All year.*

THE BELFRY COUNTRY HOTEL
Yarcombe, Near Honiton EX14 9BD
0404 86 234/588

Beautifully converted from the village school, this small licensed hotel and restaurant offers a very high standard of accommodation and food in a relaxing and peaceful atmosphere. A Grade II listed building in the centre of the hamlet of Yarcombe, once the home of Sir Francis Drake, and only one mile off the A303, it is ideally placed for touring the counties of Devon, Somerset and Dorset, and both north and south coasts. Colour brochure and details of various special interest breaks, including golf, fishing and horse riding, available on request. AA**.

£ *Any two days dinner, bed and breakfast from £68 per person (1 October 1990 to 30 April 1991), from £77 (1 May 1991 to 30 September 1991).*

SAND PEBBLES HOTEL AND RESTAURANT
Hope Cove, Near Salcombe
0548 561673/0831 218047

Sand Pebbles has been family run for nearly two decades. Situated in one of Devon's most picturesque fishing villages, with clear blue water and golden sands. Our restaurant is renowned for excellent cuisine, fine wines and freshly cooked local produce. Proprietor Maurice Hassall is a Fellow of the Hotel and Catering Association. Three hundred yards from sandy beaches, harbour and famous National Trust coastal walks. En suite rooms with beverage facilities and colour TV. Well stocked quaint old-world bar. Two comfortable lounges. Sauna bath. 'Let us spoil you.'

£ *From £30 for any one night dinner, bed and breakfast.* ✇ *March to October.*

TANFIELD HOTEL
Hope Cove, Near Kingsbridge TQ7 3HF
0548 561268

The Tanfield Hotel is Ashley Courtenay recommended and overlooks the tiny fishing village of Hope Cove. All rooms are centrally heated, en suite and have colour TV, tea/coffee making facilities and hairdryers. Pets are welcome. Hope Cove, in the South Hams, is a special corner of Devon with coastline protected by National Trust. Steep cliffs, secluded coves, beaches and panoramic views. Colour brochure and details of Special Breaks on request.

£ *Special terms for dinner, bed and breakfast for a minimum stay of 3 nights.* ☐ *Special Breaks from March to early June and from mid-September to end of October.*

LANGLEIGH COUNTRY HOTEL
Langleigh Road, Ilfracombe EX34 8EA
0271 862629

Langleigh was originally an Elizabethan manor house, then a beautiful Regency residence, and is now a small, exclusive country house hotel, set in a secluded valley. The atmosphere at Langleigh is friendly and easy-going, and children are made most welcome. Bedrooms are beautifully furnished, and all have private bathroom, colour TV, radio-intercom and tea/coffee facilities. Two self-contained cottages are available, with meals being taken at the main hotel. The town centre is only a few minutes' walk, and it is a short drive to Exmoor and the beaches.

£ ☐ *Bargain Break terms on application.*

ST BRANNOCKS HOUSE HOTEL
St Brannocks Road, Ilfracombe EX34 8EQ
0271 863873

Come and enjoy a relaxed break at St Brannocks where we offer a warm welcome and personal service. The hotel is set in its own grounds with parking space for all guests. We are within walking distance of the town, promenade and harbour. The emphasis is on comfort and good food. Enjoy a drink in the cosy, well-stocked bar or relax in the comfort of one of our separate lounges. All bedrooms are pleasantly furnished, many en suite, all with TV and tea/coffee making facilities. Access and Visa accepted.

£ *£19.50 to £23.50 per person per night for dinner, bed and breakfast. 4 night breaks from £70 to £90.* ☐ *January to December, including Christmas.*

THE CAIRNGORM HOTEL
St Brannocks Road, Ilfracombe EX34 8EH
0271 863911

The Cairngorm Hotel is delightfully situated in its own grounds with extensive views over the town, sea and surrounding countryside. All eight bedrooms are comfortably furnished, with en suite bathroom, colour television and tea/coffee making facilities. Fully centrally heated. RAC Acclaimed. AA Listed. The lounge and sun lounge overlook a picturesque park, and drinks can be enjoyed in the cosy Cottage Bar. The dining room serves a full English breakfast, and a five-course dinner with choice of traditional and Continental dishes. Diets/vegetarians catered for. Car park.

£ *From £50 for 2 nights bed, breakfast and dinner; other nights pro rata.* ☐ *All year except Bank Holidays.*

THE DARNLEY HOTEL
Belmont Road, Ilfracombe EX34 8DR
0271 863955

A small licensed hotel of charm and character, where friendly, personal service and a homely atmosphere is the prime consideration. All rooms are centrally heated and have washbasins, shaver points and comfortable beds. The proprietors, Jenny and Robin Hunt, have built their reputation on the excellent quality and quantity of food they provide. There is a colour TV lounge, a games room and a comfortable quiet lounge, as well as a cosy bar. Ilfracombe has a wide range of sports and leisure activities, and is an ideal base for touring the glorious scenery of Exmoor and North Devon.

£ *Bed and Breakfast from £14 per person.*

NYMET BRIDGE HOUSE
Lapford, Near Crediton EX17 6QX
0363 83334

Peaceful, fourteenth century country house, offering comfortable accommodation with old world charm and a reputation for good food. Set by the River Yeo, close to Eggesford Forest and Two Moors Way, in "Tarka" country where abundant wildlife delights nature lovers. Golf, fishing, riding and tennis available locally, many places of interest within easy travelling distance. Charming lounge with inglenook; oak beams throughout. Home-cooked meals served in separate dining room. Residential licence. All bedrooms have adjustable central heating and washbasins, en suite available. Regret, no children or pets.

£ *Bed and breakfast from £12, dinner £6. Short breaks 10% discount.*

COOMBE FARM
Countisbury, Lynton EX35 6NF
05987 236

Set amongst 370 acres of beautiful hill farming country, Coombe Farm dates back to the 17th century and makes an ideal base for visits to Doone Valley and Exmoor. There are two double bedrooms with en suite shower rooms; one twin and two family rooms with washbasins. All have hot drink facilities. Residential licence, Fire Certificate, central heating. Excellent country fare served in the diningroom. Children welcome. Pony trekking, fishing, golf nearby.

£ *From £24.50 to £28.00 dinner, bed and breakfast per person per night. Minimum stay 2 nights.* ◫ *April to October excluding Bank Holidays and high season.*

GABLE LODGE HOTEL
Lee Road, Lynton EX35 6BS
0598 52367

Built as a Victorian residence, Gable Lodge retains much of its original character, with a beautiful pitch pine staircase. We offer a friendly and homely atmosphere in England's "Little Switzerland", where Exmoor meets the sea. RAC Acclaimed. The twin towns of Lynton and Lynmouth, linked by the famous Cliff Railway, are an ideal spot for a relaxing holiday. Most bedrooms have en suite facilities, and all have colour TV and razor points. Good home cooking is served, with a choice of menu and an excellent wine list.

£ *£50 per person for 2 nights dinner, bed and breakfast.* ◫ *1 October to 30 November and 31 December to 31 March.*

Devon 49

ROCKVALE HOTEL
Off Lee Road, Lynton EX35 6HW
0598 52279

Delightfully situated in its own grounds, Rockvale enjoys extensive views over Lynton to Exmoor. Open most of the year, it is ideal for Spring and Autumn breaks. AA and RAC*. The attractive bedrooms are all en suite, with full central heating, colour TV, tea/coffee maker, direct-dial telephone and clock radio. There is a comfortably furnished lounge and cosy lounge bar. The varied menus served in the dining room are complemented by a specially selected wine list. There are many attractions within easy reach — ideal for walking and sightseeing.
£ *2 nights bed, breakfast and dinner £55 inc. VAT; 4 nights £107.50. Four-poster room available.* Any two nights March 1 to June 30, 1991.

THE CROWN HOTEL
Sinai Hill, Lynton EX35 6AG
0598 52253

Standing in a secluded position in one of the prettiest villages in Devon is the Crown, a former coaching inn and now a well-run modernised hotel. AA**, RAC**. Bedrooms are well appointed, with all the facilities guests would expect, and the proprietors try to ensure that all their guests' requirements are supplied. With table d'hôte and à la carte menus served in the restaurant — fresh Exmoor trout and locally caught lobsters being a speciality — and the cosy old-world beamed bar in which to relax, this is an ideal base for a short break holiday in Devon. Sea and river fishing and walks nearby.
£ *From £27 per person per day for dinner, bed and breakfast. Minimum stay two nights.* All year.

LUNDY HOUSE HOTEL
Chapel Hill, Mortehoe EX34 7DZ
0271 870372

Small, friendly private hotel midway between Mortehoe and Woolacombe, with gardens adjoining the rugged coastal path, access to beach and spectacular sea views to Lundy Island. The hotel serves traditional home cooking and benefits from gas central heating, comfortable licensed bar lounge, en suite bathrooms and showers. Parking. Open from February to October and ideal for walking, rambling or visiting Exmoor and local beauty spots. For colour brochure and tariff, please write or telephone now.
£ *£69 per person for any 3 nights, full English breakfast and 4 course dinner.* February to May and September to October.

STOWFORD HOUSE HOTEL
Lewdown, Okehampton EX20 4BZ
056-683 415

Stowford House Hotel, a former old rectory, offers a warm welcome, comfortable rooms, interesting food and a tranquil garden. Perfect for a complete rest or as a convenient holiday centre. Peaceful setting, within easy reach of beautiful Dartmoor and Lydford Gorge and ideal for touring North and South Devon and Cornwall. Single, double and family rooms available, most with en suite facilities. Children over five years of age welcome. Sorry, no dogs allowed inside the hotel. Guests are assured of a friendly, homely atmosphere and superb food, freshly prepared from the finest ingredients. RAC and AA Listed, "Staying off the Beaten Track".
£ *3 day break (Mon-Thurs). Dinner, bed and breakfast £80.*

FLUXTON FARM
Ottery St Mary EX11 1RJ
0404 812818

This lovely 16th century farmhouse situated in 2 acres of gardens including stream, trout pond, putting green and garden railway is in the Otter Valley only five miles from the beach at Sidmouth. Delicious home cooking using fresh local produce is served in the beamed, candlelit diningroom. Licensed. AA Listed, Ashley Courtenay Recommended. Two lounges with colour TV; one non-smoking. Log fires. The bedrooms, all double rooms en suite, have teasmades and are centrally heated. Children and pets welcome. Parking.

£ *2 day break from £48 (October-April), £52 (May-September) for dinner, bed and breakfast.*

TORBAY HOLIDAY MOTEL
Dept. SB, Totnes Road, Paignton TQ4 7PP
0803 558226

Comfortable modern motel set in country surroundings close to Torbay. AA** RAC**. Each of the 16 bedrooms has en suite facilities with shower, telephone, colour TV, and tea and coffee making facilities. Excellent restaurant, and bar. Facilities for guests include a mini-gym with sauna and solarium, heated indoor and outdoor pool, crazy golf, and an adventure playground. Ideal touring centre.

£ *£23-£26 per person per night for one or more nights table d'hôte dinner, bed and full English breakfast; including VAT. 10% discount for senior citizens except June/July/August.* ☐ *All year except 24-31 December.*

HERON HOUSE HOTEL
Thurlestone Sands, Salcombe
0548 561308

Situated at the edge of the sea, 50 yards off the beach and on the coastal path, this friendly, family-run hotel enjoys stunning coastal and rural views. Probably the finest location to be found. All 18 beautifully appointed bedrooms are en suite, with colour TV, tea-making facilities and direct-dial telephone. Ashley Courtenay recommended. There is a large outdoor swimming pool, heated May to September. The Proprietor personally supervises the first class cuisine, specialising in Devon produce. Guests can relax in the comfortable bar lounge and separate quiet lounge.

£ *Terms on application for off-season breaks.*

ORCHARDSIDE HOTEL
Cotford Road, Sidbury, Near Sidmouth EX10 0SQ
03957 351

This delightful small country hotel and restaurant stands in an acre of lovely gardens, with panoramic views of the countryside. It is situated on the edge of the lovely unspoilt village of Sidbury, only two and a half miles from the sea. This is ideal walking country, with opportunities too for golf, fishing and horse riding. All the well-furnished bedrooms have tea/coffee making facilities, colour TV and central heating, and most have showers en suite. The restaurant offers a good choice of menu and a full bar. Large car park.

£ *Dinner, bed and breakfast from £25.00 per person per night. Bed and breakfast from £15.00 per person.* ☐ *All year.*

Devon 51

BABBACOMBE CLIFF HOTEL
Torbay

One of the best positioned hotels in Torbay. Set in two-and-a-half acres of private grounds, with panoramic sea views. All rooms are en suite, with colour TV and tea-making facilities. Other amenities include a restaurant, bar and swimming pool. Conveniently situated just minutes from shops, theatre and beach. For full colour brochure ring Cardiff (0222) 398673.

£ Bargain Breaks £55 for 3 days, longer breaks pro rata. Includes full English breakfast and evening meal.
🗓 January to December.

BELVEDERE HOUSE HOTEL
Braddons Hill Road West, Torquay TQ1 1BG
0803 293313

Located above the inner harbour, this Grade II Listed building, built for the Cary family, is now a comfortable hotel. AA**. All bedrooms are en suite, and have colour TV and tea-making facilities; there is also a comfortable lounge and cosy bar. Belvedere House is convenient for shops, theatres, cinemas and other attractions, and the small lawned garden has lovely views over the Bay. The mild climate of this area makes it ideal for a short break at any time of the year. Colour brochure available on request. Children over 10 years.

£ From £28.00 per person (with sea-view room when available).

HIND HOTEL
29 Bampfylde Road, Torquay TQ2 5AY
0803 297212/297708

A family-run hotel offering a high standard of food, service and accommodation, situated a short, level walk from the sea front and Leisure Centre. Town centre is within easy reach. There are 12 comfortable bedrooms, all en suite and with tea-making facilities and colour TVs. The hotel offers a full English breakfast and four-course Evening Dinner, and for guests to relax in there is a sun terrace, pleasant bar, and quiet lounge. The Hind provides a convenient holiday base. Access & Visa.

£ 2 nights bed and breakfast — £32; bed, breakfast and evening dinner — £46 (10% reduction for Senior Citizens). 🗓 5th October to December; January to April (except Bank Holidays).

KISTOR HOTEL
Belgrave Road, Torquay TQ2 5HF
0803 212632 Fax: 0803 293219

A relaxed 3 star hotel, open all year. It is levelly situated close to beach, parks, and country walks. Nearby is the leisure centre and shops. All rooms en suite, with tea-making, TV, radio and telephone. There is an indoor pool, spa bath, sauna and solarium, music/dancing up to 3 nights during most weeks of the year. Bookings from any day to any day, all fully inclusive, Full Board, Dinner, Room and Breakfast or Room and Breakfast terms. Short Breaks and residential conference/meeting terms. Four poster 'Celebration' Room at this 4 Crown Hotel.

£ 2 nights full board from £64 to £80 per person. 🗓 14 September 1990 to 7 April 1992, excluding Christmas, New Year and Easter.

NORCLIFFE HOTEL
Babbacombe Downs Road, Torquay
0803 328456

A traditional, family run hotel with 22 bedrooms, all en suite. AA**, RAC**. All rooms have colour TV, radio, direct-dial telephone, tea making facilities, and all are centrally heated. There is a licensed bar and restaurant offering delicious five course menus. The hotel overlooks the sea and has an attractive elevated sea front garden. Lounges are spacious and comfortable, and the attractive diningroom enjoys glorious views over Lyme Bay. It is ideally placed on Babbacombe Downs. Colour brochure on request from resident proprietors Jean and John Farrell.

£ *From £15 per day for bed and breakfast; from £24 with dinner.* ☐ *All year.*

WOODY BAY HOTEL
Woody Bay, Parracombe EX31 4QX
059-83 264

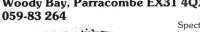

Spectacularly set on a wooded hillside above Woody Bay, the hotel offers magnificent views over the coastline and is ideal for those seeking comfort, interesting food, and the tranquillity that is Exmoor. A wide selection of hot and cold bar lunches is always available, and the outstanding reputation of the restaurant, offering both table d'hôte and à la carte in the evenings, makes booking in advance desirable. A perfect hideaway from busy roads and overcrowded resorts while enjoying the delights of Devon. Ashley Courtenay, Relais Routiers, Egon Ronay recommended.

£ *From £72 per person for two nights dinner, bed and breakfast. Extra nights pro rata.* ☐ *November to March.*

PEBBLES HOTEL AND RESTAURANT
Chapel Hill, Mortehoe, Woolacombe EX34 7EA
0271 870426

Pebbles boasts magnificent views from its National Trust land setting, and is literally a stone's throw from the beach. AA recommended. Golf, fishing, riding and shooting arranged for the energetic and there are two superb licensed restaurants, a well stocked bar and a beautifully appointed conservatory. All 12 bedrooms are en suite and have TV, tea/coffee making facilities, radio and baby listening.

£ *From £65 per person for weekend breaks, including two nights bed and breakfast, plus one meal in à la carte restaurant, one in the carvery and Sunday lunch. Extra days on bed and breakfast basis from £18 per person.* ☐ *All year.*

WOOLACOMBE BAY HOTEL
Woolacombe EX34 7BN
0271 870388

Simply the best. An elegant hotel open from February to early January. Ideal for quiet weekends or mid-week breaks, as well as the traditional summer holiday. Perfect for the traditional Christmas holiday. Restful holidays or action-packed excitement — the choice is yours. Abounding with free sporting facilities including heated swimming pool, squash, tennis, solarium, areobics, aquarobics, pitch and putt, billiards, short-mat bowling and much more. Write for brochure from Mr S. B. Holiday.

£ *Weekend breaks; dinner, bed and breakfast.* ☐ *September to mid-December; February to mid-July.*

Devon 53

Dorset

LA BELLE ALLIANCE
White Cliff Mill Street, Blandford DT11 7BP
0258 452842

La Belle Alliance is, uniquely, a French-style country restaurant with bedrooms and offers gourmet breaks — superb food and wine in the most comfortable surroundings. Its atmosphere is one of unobtrusive good taste, enhanced by antique furniture and decoration. An aperitif may be enjoyed in the lounge before dinner and food is, of course, of the finest quality. Ideal for New Forest and Dorset coast. Recommended by all leading restaurant guides and is the only restaurant in Dorset to be commended by the BTA.

£ *Short gourmet breaks available from £82 per person for two nights dinner, bed and breakfast.* All year.

Hinton Firs
BOURNEMOUTH

INDOOR AND OUTDOOR POOLS

In the heart of the East Cliff, set amongst rhododendrons and pine trees, our friendly family hotel has 4 lounges facing sheltered gardens and sun terrace.

- All 52 Rooms incl. 12 Singles, with Bath or Shower
- TV, Radio, Tea-making and Direct-Dial Telephone in every room
- Dancing • Games Room • Sauna
- Indoor and Outdoor Pools • Spa Pool
- Bar Lunches • Children's Teas
- Lift • Car Parking • Night Porter

AA
★★★

ASHLEY COURTENAY RECOMMENDED

Colour Brochure from **Mr & Mrs R.J. Waters**
**Hinton Firs (RSBH 91), Manor Road,
East Cliff, Bournemouth BH1 3HB
Tel: (0202) 555409**

THE KNOLL HOUSE

A COUNTRY HOUSE HOTEL

- Within a National Trust reserve – overlooking three miles of golden beach and native heath.
- An independent country-house hotel under the third generation of personal owner management. A civilised and relaxing holiday for all ages.
- Six fine lounges and restaurant; tennis courts, nine acre golf course and outdoor heated pool. Jacuzzi, sauna, Turkish room, plunge-pool and gym.
- Family suites, two games rooms, separate young children's restaurant, playroom and fabulous SAFE adventure playground.
- The many ground-floor and single rooms are a popular all-age asset, rare in most hotels.
- Daily full board terms: £45-£63 incl. VAT and service Children's terms according to age.

Open Easter - end of October 1991
STUDLAND BAY DORSET
BH19 3AE
092 944 251

ANVIL HOTEL AND RESTAURANT
Pimperne, Blandford DT11 8UQ
0258 453431/480182

A long, low thatched building set in a tiny village deep in the Dorset countryside — what could be more English? And that is what visitors to the Anvil will find — a typical old English hostelry offering good, old-fashioned English hospitality. A full à la carte menu is available in the charming beamed and flagged restaurant, and a wide selection of bar meals in the attractive, fully licensed bar. All bedrooms have private facilities. Ample parking. RAC**, AA**.

£ *From £80 for two persons for two nights bed and breakfast.* ○ *October to May, except Bank Holidays.*

CATHERINGTON HOUSE HOTEL
38 Parkwood Road, Bournemouth
0202 428521

Delightfully situated family-run hotel of character close to Bournemouth's beach and shops. All bedrooms are en suite with colour television and telephone, and all have tea and coffee making facilities. We are noted for our high standard of accommodation and excellent food (table licence). The attractions of Dorset's lovely country and famous coast lie within easy reach. Access, Visa, Diners Club, and American Express accepted.

£ *£50 per person for two nights dinner, bed and breakfast. Extra nights pro rata.* ○ *Mid-September to 31 March.*

CHESTERWOOD HOTEL
East Overcliff, Bournemouth BH1 3AR
0202 558057

Elegant 3 star hotel, ideally situated in a fine cliff top position, overlooking the bay yet within minutes from the town centre. AA and RAC***. All rooms en suite with tea/coffee, direct-dial telephones, colour TV, radio and hair dryers. Licensed bar, heated outdoor swimming pool (May-September), own car parking. Seasonal entertainment. Limited free golf on municipal course.

£ *Any two nights dinner, bed and full English breakfast from £56.00 per person sharing twin room.*
⌕ *October 1990 to March 1991 (excluding Christmas and New Year).*

FRESHFIELDS HOTEL
55 Christchurch Road, Bournemouth BH1 3DA
0202 394023

Freshfields is a small licensed hotel close to the sea, shops and all the other amenities of Bournemouth and Boscombe. Boscombe Pier and beach are about 4 minutes' walk; rail station, bus depots and Bournemouth International Centre are close by. All rooms have central heating, colour TV and tea-making facilities, and there is a comfortable lounge with colour TV and a dining room with separate tables. En suite rooms available. Full fire certificate. Access at all times with own keys. ETB Commended, Les Routiers.

£ *Bed and breakfast only, from £13. Bargain breaks — 10% off 3 nights or more. Special offers 23 September to 15 June. Also 10% off weekly bookings throughout the year.*

HINTON FIRS HOTEL
Manor Road, East Cliff, Bournemouth BH1 3HB
0202 555409

Hinton Firs is a warm and friendly hotel situated near the seafront in the well-known holiday resort of Bournemouth. Four sunny lounges face south onto the sun trap terrace and sheltered gardens. Other amenities include a sauna, indoor and outdoor pools, and a spa pool. All bedrooms have bath or shower, TV, radio, tea-making facilities and direct-dial telephone. AA***. Set amongst rhododendrons and pine trees, this family-run hotel is ideal for a break at any time of year. "Super Bargain" breaks available December and January.

£ *Dinner, bed and breakfast from £29.50 per person per night. 2 nights minimum, additional nights pro rata. No supplement for singles.* ⌕ *2 November 1990 to 7 May 1991, excluding Christmas, New Year and Easter.*

LANGTRY MANOR HOTEL
Derby Road, East Cliff, Bournemouth BH1 3QB
0202 23887

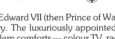

Langtry Manor was built by Edward VII (then Prince of Wales) for his mistress Lillie Langtry. The luxuriously appointed en suite bedrooms have all modern comforts — colour TV, radio, direct-dial telephone and mini-bar. Sumptuous four-poster suites are available for that really special occasion. The hotel is renowned for the standard of its menus, complemented by a selection of fine wines. This high quality cuisine and accommodation is matched by the attentive and friendly service. RAC and AA***. On Saturday evenings there is a six-course Edwardian dinner party.

£ *Dinner, bed and breakfast from £49.50 per person per night (supplements for four-poster rooms).* ⌕ *All year.*

NORFOLK ROYALE HOTEL
Richmond Hill, Bournemouth BH2 6EN
0202 551521

Set in the heart of Bournemouth, this luxurious, Edwardian-styled hotel blends the best in traditional comforts with modern amenities. Residents are offered free use of the leisure facilities, which include a pool, spa, steam room and sauna, and secure parking. All bedrooms are exceptionally well-appointed and have satellite TV, in-room movies and mini-bar. AA/RAC **** Deluxe.

[£] *Royale Break: includes à la carte meals in the Peacock gourmet restaurant with wine cellar. Dinner, bed and breakfast from £65 per person per night. Norfolk Break: includes dinner in Orangery restaurant (ideal for families) with table d'hôte menu. Dinner, bed and breakfast from £52.50 per person per night.* All year.

TRALEE HOTEL
West Cliff, Bournemouth BH2 5EQ
0202 556246 Fax: 0202 295229

There's so much more to enjoy at the Tralee whether it's your main summer holiday, a weekend break with the family or just a relaxing few days away together. All 90 bedrooms are well appointed, with colour satellite TV, telephone, radio and tea/coffee tray. Other attractions include an indoor heated swimming pool, sauna, solarium, games room, beauty salon and dancing. Superb cliff top position, close to town centre for shops, shows and leisure centre.

[£] *Two nights dinner, bed and breakfast in double or twin room with private facilities £69.50.* November 1990 to April 1991.

Swanage Beach, looking towards the Pier and Peveril Point, Dorset.

Dorset 57

ULLSWATER HOTEL
Westcliff Gardens, Bournemouth BH2 5HW
0202 555181

Within sight of the sea and situated in the most favoured position on the Westcliff. Sheltered and quiet, yet only a few minutes' walking distance of the beach, town centre, shops and entertainment. The hotel is conveniently situated close to the Bournemouth International Centre. Recently refurbished throughout, all rooms are en suite, with colour TV, radio, direct-dial telephone and tea/coffee making facilities. Licensed cocktail bar, comfortable lounges, free car parking, regular dancing and entertainment, snooker room, table tennis. Full central heating. Good food and personal service from resident proprietors.

£ *Weekend/midweek breaks from £42 per person (inc. VAT) for 2 nights dinner, bed and breakfast.* ▢ *All year except Christmas and Easter.*

YALBURY COTTAGE
Lower Bockhampton, Dorchester DT2 8PZ
0305 262382

Thatched Grade II Listed hotel. Eight beautifully appointed en suite bedrooms providing every comfort, including colour TV, telephone, tea/coffee facilities, ironing centre, hairdryer, bathrobes etc. The spacious bedrooms, and public rooms complete with beams and inglenook fireplaces, create an atmosphere of peace and tranquillity. The restaurant with its long-standing reputation for excellence provides the perfect complement to the relaxed and welcoming atmosphere of the hotel. Ideal for mini breaks.

£ *Special Winter breaks.* ▢ *Open January to December.*

THE KNOLL HOUSE
Studland BH19 3HE
092-944 251

The Knoll House is a family run country hotel in the wonderful coastal setting of a National Trust reserve overlooking three miles of golden beach and native heath. AA***, RAC***. The hotel offers excellent facilities for all ages, with six fine lounges and restaurant, tennis courts, nine-acre golf course, and outdoor heated pool; Jacuzzi, sauna, steam rooms, plunge pool, and gym. For the children there is a restaurant, playroom, adventure playground, and two games rooms, as well as family suites.

£ *£218 per person for five nights full board in double/twin room with washbasin; £654 for family suite with two adults and two children.* ▢ *Out of season.*

THE LIMES HOTEL
48 Park Road, Swanage BH19 2AE
0929 422664

The Limes is a friendly family hotel which offers excellent home cooking. Centrally heated, it has a licensed bar, games room and children's play garden. ETB Listed. All rooms have TV and tea/coffee facilities. This is an ideal base for ramblers, with the coastal path and National Trust attractions close by for all lovers of the unspoiled English countryside. Historic Dorchester and Salisbury and many historic houses are close by, and Bournemouth with excellent shops, theatres and clubs is just 5 miles away.

£ *3 nights bed, breakfast and evening meal £70 per person, reductions for children. Christmas — adults only — £200 for 3 nights full board.* ▢ *All year except July and August.*

58 *Dorset*

Durham

MORRITT ARMS HOTEL
Barnard Castle DL12 9SE
0833 27232 27392

The Morritt Arms Hotel is a privately run country house hotel with a traditional atmosphere, and has associations with Sir Walter Scott and Charles Dickens. The bar has world famous Dickensian murals on its walls. The lounge has an open log fire and the restaurant can seat 38 people. There are 17 bedrooms, all with en suite facilities. Bedrooms have direct-dial telephones. Dogs welcome. No background music.

£ *2 nights dinner, bed and breakfast per person £80 (1st April to 31st October 1990), £70 (1st November 1990 to 31st March 1991). Extra nights pro rata. Single room supplement.*

BRIDGE TOBY HOTEL
Croxdale, Durham
091-378 0524

The Bridge Toby Hotel is in an ideal location for touring and among the places of interest are Hadrian's Wall, Holy Island, Durham Dales and, of course, historic Durham with its Norman cathedral and castle. All 46 bedrooms have en suite facilities, colour TV, trouser press and tea/coffee making equipment. Bar and popular Toby Grill Restaurant.

£ *Two nights stay on weekend, bed and breakfast only £21.50 per person per night, with a £3 single supplement. All year.*

TEESDALE HOTEL
Middleton-in-Teesdale
0833 40264

A mullioned-windowed former coaching inn, the Teesdale Hotel has been transformed into a comfortable hotel by owners Mr and Mrs Streit. RAC**, AA** and Red Star Award. The hotel has a welcoming atmosphere redolent of unhurried days, yet facilities have been skilfully modernised. Bedrooms are warm and comfortable, and guests are assured of good home cooking complemented by an excellent wine list. This is a perfect place from which to explore the moors, hills, and dales of Durham and North Yorkshire.

£ *2 nights dinner, bed and breakfast: until 31.1.91 (excluding Bank Holidays) £68.50 per person, from 1.2.91 to 30.4.91 from £69 to £72.50.*

Essex

NEW WORLD HOTEL
Great Warley Street, Warley, Brentwood
0277 226418/220483 Fax: 0277 229795

A Tudor-style manor house situated in the heart of the undulating Essex countryside, within 3 minutes of London Orbital Motorway. ETB. All guest rooms, some of family size, have colour television, shower, telephone and valet trouser press, while room service operates for 18 hours a day. Excellent à la carte and table d'hôte meals are served in the Elizabethan candlelit restaurant, and there are three spacious bars. The hotel has 12 acres of gardens with a heated swimming pool and diversions for children, plus a fully-equipped health and leisure club. 2 tennis courts. Golf, fishing and riding nearby.
£ *From £27 per night single room, £35 double room. Breaks comprise three nights Friday, Saturday and Sunday bed and full English breakfast.* ☐ *All year.*

Ramsey Windmill, Essex.

Gloucestershire

COTSWOLDS
Bourton-on-the-Water / Stow-on-the-Wold

The **Cotswold Stone Cottages** below are on the outskirts of the small historic market town of Stow-on-the-Wold near Bourton-on-the-Water in the heart of the Cotswolds. They have been tastefully modernised and decorated and are comfortably furnished complete with colour television and central heating. Open all year. Pets permitted.
Winter Weekends from £58 per cottage October to April.
Charming 17th Century Cottage with a wealth of oak beams and two inglenook fireplaces. Sleeps 6.
Lovely 17th Century Cottage with beamed ceilings and inglenook. Sleeps 3/4.
Quaint Little Old Cottage heated by log fire. Sleeps 2.
Tiny One-Bedroomed Old World Cottage Sleeps 1/2.
Please phone or write for further details and illustrated brochure.
Mrs. S. Harrison, Olive Hill Farm, Wyck Rissington, Bourton-on-the-Water GL54 2PW.
Telephone: Cotswold (0451) 20350.

COTSWOLDS 1991
GETAWAY BREAKS

Colesbourne Inn
Near Cheltenham, Gloucestershire
Tel: (024 287) 376   Fax: (024 287) 397

* En Suite Bedroom   * Full English Breakfast
* 3 Course à la carte Dinner   *Coffee

2 NIGHTS £75 per person
3 NIGHTS £110 per person
4 NIGHTS £135 per person
(Sharing Twin or Double Room)
Situated on A435 twixt Cheltenham & Cirencester

AA Specially Selected Inn   Les Routiers
RAC Two Tankard   Good Beer Guide
Egon Ronay Recommended   ETB ♛♛♛ Commended

BIBURY COURT HOTEL
Bibury GL7 5NT
028-574 337 Fax: 0285 74660

Bibury Court is a beautiful old mansion originally dating from Tudor times. A picturesque setting in six acres of grounds beside River Coln. Dry fly trout fishing in garden. Other facilities nearby include golf and riding. AA, RAC. The atmosphere is one of tranquillity, relaxation, and good living, with an absence of formality. Direct dial telephone and colour TV in all bedrooms. Bibury Court provides excellent accommodation, food, and wine, and is an excellent base from which to tour the Cotswolds, Stratford, Oxford, Cheltenham, and Bath.

£ *From £90 per person for two nights dinner, bed and Continental breakfast.* ◘ *1 Nov.–31 March (except Cheltenham Festival week). Closed Christmas, open New Year.*

LOWER VINEY COUNTRY GUEST HOUSE
Viney Hill, Blakeney GL15 4LT
0594 516000

At Viney Hill between the Royal Forest of Dean and the River Severn Estuary is a most delightful period farmhouse, set in gardens of approximately half an acre with extensive views over the surrounding countryside. Beautifully situated in a very special part of England, it offers easy access to the cathedral cities of Hereford, Gloucester and Worcester, the Welsh Borders and many other places of interest. All rooms have tea/coffee facilities; guest lounge with colour TV; separate dining room; central heating. Lower Viney offers quality accommodation with friendly service.

£ *2 nights bed, breakfast and evening meal £52.00 per person; extra night plus evening meal £26.* ◘ *Mid week only, all year except Bank Holiday weeks.*

OLIVE HILL FARM
Wyck Rissington, Bourton-on-the-Water GL54 2PW
0451 20350

The following Cotswold Stone Cottages are on the outskirts of the small historic market town of Stow-on-the-Wold, near Bourton-on-the-Water in the heart of the Cotswolds. Charming 17th century cottage with a wealth of oak beams, sleeps 6, also lovely 17th century cottage sleeps 3/4, quaint little cottage sleeping 2, and a tiny one bedroomed cottage are available. They have been tastefully modernised and decorated and are comfortably furnished, complete with colour television and central heating. Pets allowed.

£ *Winter weekends from £58 per cottage.* ◘ *October to April.*

THE COLESBOURNE INN
Colesbourne, Near Cheltenham GL53 9NP
0242-87 376

The 200 year old inn, situated in the Cotswold countryside, retains all its traditional charm while offering guests a high standard of comfort and service. RAC, AA, Egon Ronay. All bedrooms have en suite facilities, colour TV, telephone and tea making facilities. Home grown produce used in the restaurant, while the bar has local ale and real log fires. Golf available in the area; ideal for walking and exploring Cotswolds by car. Large car park. You will get a warm welcome and super food!

£ *2 nights bed, breakfast and evening meal – £75 per person. 3 nights £110, 4 nights £135.* ◘ *All year.*

CHARINGWORTH MANOR
Charingworth, Near Chipping Campden GL55 6NS
038-678 555 Fax: 038-678 353

The ancient manor of Charingworth, first mentioned in the Domesday Book of 1086, lies in its own estate surrounded by the gently rolling Cotswold countryside. Here guests can enjoy peace, tranquillity and breathtaking views. The 25 bedrooms offer every comfort, with antiques and fine fabrics throughout. Chef Tony Robson Burrell's award-winning cooking is complemented by a good wine list. Charingworth is ideally situated for exploring the "Heart of England", with many places of interest in the surrounding countryside, and the picturesque towns of Chipping Campden and Stratford-upon-Avon only a few miles away. RAC Blue Ribbon, AA Best New Hotel 1988/9.

£ *From £66-£72 per person per night for dinner, bed and breakfast. Minimum 2 nights stay, double occupancy.* Excl. Xmas, New Year, Bank Holidays and Cheltenham Gold Cup Week.

WILD DUCK INN
Ewen, Near Cirencester GL7 6BY
0285 770310/770364

Dating from 1563, the Wild Duck Inn offers traditional comfort combined with modern amenities. RAC***; Egon Ronay, Ashley Courtenay. The inn has nine comfortable and well fitted bedrooms, all en suite, two of which have four poster beds and overlook the award-winning garden. Guests may also relax in the Grouse room lounge with its Elizabethan inglenook fireplace. The restaurant has an extensive menu and is renowned for its excellent cuisine and fine selection of good wines, while bar meals and morning coffee can be enjoyed in the beamed Post Horn bar.

£ *From £80 per room inc. dinner, bed, breakfast. Break to include Saturday night.* All year.

FOR THE MUTUAL GUIDANCE OF GUEST AND HOST

Every year literally thousands of holidays, short-breaks and overnight stops are arranged through our guides, the vast majority without any problems at all. In a handful of cases, however, difficulties do arise about bookings, which often could have been prevented from the outset.

It is important to remember that when accommodation has been booked, both parties — guests and hosts — have entered into a form of contract. We hope that the following points will provide helpful guidance.

GUESTS: When enquiring about accommodation, be as precise as possible. Give exact dates, numbers in your party and the ages of any children. State the number and type of rooms wanted and also what catering you require — bed and breakfast, full board, etc. Make sure that the position about evening meals is clear — and about pets, reductions for children or any other special points.

Read our reviews carefully to ensure that the proprietors you are going to contact can supply what you want. Ask for a letter confirming all arrangements, if possible.

If you have to cancel, do so as soon as possible. Proprietors do have the right to retain deposits and under certain circumstances to charge for cancelled holidays if adequate notice is not given and they cannot re-let the accommodation.

HOSTS: Give details about your facilities and about any special conditions. Explain your deposit system clearly and arrangements for cancellations, charges, etc, and whether or not your terms include VAT.

If for any reason you are unable to fulfil an agreed booking without adequate notice, you may be under an obligation to arrange alternative suitable accommodation or to make some form of compensation.

While every effort is made to ensure accuracy, we regret that FHG Publications cannot accept responsibility for errors, omissions or misrepresentation in our entries or any consequences thereof. Prices in particular should be checked because we go to press early. We will follow up complaints but cannot act as arbiters or agents for either party.

Gloucestershire 63

Hampshire

THE MILBURY'S
Beauworth, Cheriton SO24 0PB
0962 79248

Full of character and old world charm, the Milbury's is situated 6 miles east of Winchester, off the A272 Petersfield Road. The family room of this historic free house boasts a 300ft deep well and a 24ft treadmill. The beautiful French restaurant is renowned for its superb à la carte menu, and a wide range of bar food is available at reasonable prices. Accommodation is of the same high standard, and includes a family suite.

£ *Friday night to Sunday brunch, with evening meals included — £60 per person.*

RHINEFIELD HOUSE HOTEL
Rhinefield Road, Brockenhurst SO42 7QB
0590 22922

A magnificent Victorian house standing in its own restored gardens and surrounded by the lovely New Forest, Rhinefield is perfect for a break from the town or from crowded resorts. Bedrooms are well appointed with all facilities, and there is a leisure centre and tennis and croquet. Relax in the Lounge Bar or Armada Restaurant which serves à la carte meals or, if you prefer, just a drink. Guests are also intriguingly promised, as a feature, the Lost City of Atlantis.

£ **£100 per person for two nights dinner, bed and breakfast. Based on two persons sharing, subject to availability. Special offers in January and February.** *All year.*

BARTLEY LODGE HOTEL
Cadnam, New Forest, Southampton SO4 2NR
0703 812248

This fine Listed building, built in 1759, today stands in perfect condition in the heart of the New Forest. AA/RAC***. Ashley Courtenay Recommended. Many of the 19 bedrooms enjoy views of the lake and grounds, which include a covered heated swimming pool and two all-weather tennis courts. The accommodation is of a very high standard, and all bedrooms are en suite, with colour television, direct-dial telephone and tea/coffee making facilities. Bartley Lodge is a most civilised retreat in a rural setting, combining the best of today with the charm of yesterday.

£ *Dinner, bed and breakfast: 2 nights £85, 3 nights £120. Terms based on 2 adults sharing a deluxe double.*

HIGH CORNER INN
Linwood, Near Ringwood BH24 3QY
0425 473973

This lovely, typically English, early 18th century inn lies in the very heart of the New Forest. Its unique setting, completely surrounded by forest, makes it a haven of peace and tranquillity with many glorious walks all around. Amenities include a squash court and stables and a self-catering woodland chalet – guests can bring their own horse if they wish. All bedrooms have en suite facilities and TV. A lunchtime choice can be made from the wide-ranging bar menu, and in the evenings the charming little restaurant serves a tempting à la carte menu. Egon Ronay, Good Pub Guide, Les Routiers.

£ *Any two nights bed and full breakfast £60 per person.* 3 September 1990 to 31 May 1991 excluding Bank Holidays.

KARELIA HOLIDAYS
The Studio, Ashley, Ringwood BH24 2EE
0425 478920

Three Finnish log houses and a cottage, Tourist Board Approved, standing in private grounds of 4 acres of mature woodland, backing onto Ringwood Forest. All properties, equipped to highest standards, have private gardens and built-in barbecues. The lodges sleep from 5 to 10 persons; cottage sleeps 6. All have well-equipped kitchens and colour TV. Bed linen can be hired; electricity by slot meter. Storage heaters in winter included in terms. Games room available at small charge, also traditional Finnish log sauna and swimming pool. Pets welcome at small charge.

£ *3 night breaks available from £80 (15 October 1990–25 May 1991); Christmas Breaks and Bank Holidays from £140.*

LITTLE FOREST LODGE HOTEL
Poulner Hill, Ringwood BH24 3HS
0425 478848

A luxurious country house hotel set in three acres, one mile from Ringwood in beautiful countryside. AA selected, RAC acclaimed. All bedrooms are en suite offering colour television and tea and coffee making facilities. High standard of cuisine. Oak-panelled diningroom looks out over three acres of landscaped gardens. The residential bar and elegant lounge offer the warmth and comfort of a log fire during winter months. Golf, fishing, riding and sailing available locally. An ideal location for visiting Salisbury, Romsey and Winchester. Brochure on request from Eric and Jane Martin.

£ *From £55 per person for two nights dinner, bed and breakfast.* 1 October to 17 May.

EXPLANATION OF SYMBOLS

TA	Travel Agency Commission
♛	Number of Crowns
⚿	Number of Keys
🐕	Pets Welcome
🪆	Reductions for Children
♿	Suitable for Disabled
🌲	Christmas Breaks

Hampshire 65

Herefordshire

THE BOWENS COUNTRY HOUSE
Fownhope HR1 4PS
043277 430

Delightful Georgian farmhouse providing high standard accommodation with en suite facilities, including four ground floor bedrooms, full central heating and log fires. Tea trays and colour TV throughout. Peacefully situated with large attractive garden with putting green and grass tennis court. Situated in the Wye Valley (Area of Outstanding Natural Beauty), with glorious views. This is the perfect centre for walking/touring the Welsh Marches, Malverns, Forest of Dean etc. Excellent home cooking using own fresh/local produce daily; vegetarians welcome. Access and Visa accepted. AA Listed. Residential licence.

£ *Bed and breakfast from £17.00; dinner, bed and breakfast from £26.50. Special weekly terms — Bargain Breaks.* ⓒ *All year.*

YE OLDE TALBOT HOTEL
New Street, Ledbury HR8 2DX
0531 2963

Relax in England's most romantic town at the historic Talbot Hotel and dine by candlelight in the Old Oak Room with its original Jacobean carvings and panelling complete with bullet holes caused during a skirmish between Cavaliers and Roundheads in 1645. Now much more peaceful, the Talbot has seven tastefully furnished oak beamed bedrooms and resident owners dedicated to your comfort and enjoyment. Log fires, real ales and good service complete your pleasure. AA**, Egon Ronay Good Food Inn. Write or phone for brochure. Bar snacks and grills served lunchtimes and evenings until 9pm.

£ *Terms on application.*

HIGHFIELD
Newtown, Ivington Road, Leominster HR6 8QD
0568 3216 (changing in 1991 to 0568 613216)

Commended

Elegant Edwardian house in one acre of garden surrounded by fields and hills. Three double bedrooms, charmingly decorated, one with en suite bathroom. The other two rooms share a bathroom/toilet and a shower/toilet. All rooms have tea and coffee making facilities. There is a television lounge and the hotel has a residential licence. Delicious home cooking.

£ *Weekend Breaks £26 per person per night with en suite room, dinner, bed and breakfast. Extra nights pro rata.* ⓒ *All year.*

CROWN HOTEL
Whitchurch, Near Ross-on-Wye HR9 6DB
0600 890234

A 16th century coaching house set in the Wye Valley a quarter mile from Symonds Yat. AA, RAC listed. Rooms retain their original character, with oak beams, and log fires in the bar and function room. All bedrooms are en suite with tea/coffee making facilities, TV and full central heating. Four-posters in some rooms. Chef proprietor provides excellent bar meals seven days a week; table d'hôte and à la carte menu is available in the evenings. Skittle alley and pool room. The Crown is ideal for a walking or touring break. Diners, Amex, Visa, Access accepted.

£ **£44 per person for two nights dinner, bed and breakfast. Three nights £65; seven nights £150.** ☐ *All year except Christmas. SAE for brochure.*

GLEWSTONE COURT HOTEL
Glewstone, Near Ross-on-Wye HR9 6AW
098-984 367

Christine and William Reeve-Tucker fell in love with this 250-year-old manor in 1987. Surrounded by pretty gardens and fruit orchards, it is now their family home and charming country house hotel, offering informal service and warm hospitality. Bedrooms are spacious and tasteful furnishings throughout provide comfort while complementing the character of the house. An imaginative menu using seasonal local produce is offered in the popular restaurant. Among other activities, adventurous guests can arrange a balloon flight from the grounds. AA** Commended. Tourist Board Award.

£ *Two nights, bed, breakfast and dinner from £85 per person.*
☐ *Not Bank Holidays, Christmas or Cheltenham Gold Cup.*

THE ARCHES COUNTRY HOUSE
Walford Road, Ross-on-Wye HR9 5PT
0989 63348

Attractive Georgian-style, family-run hotel set in half an acre of lawns. Ideally situated only 10 minutes' walk from town centre. All bedrooms are furnished and decorated to a high standard and have views of the lawned garden. Bedrooms have tea/coffee facilities and colour TV. There is an attractive residents' lounge with colour TV. Full central heating; ample parking in grounds. The Arches is renowned for good food and a warm, friendly atmosphere with personal service. Children at reduced rates sharing; generous weekly reductions. Open all year except Christmas. AA Listed, RAC Acclaimed, Les Routiers Award.

£ *Bed and breakfast from £28 per person for 2 nights; dinner, bed and breakfast £46 per person for 2 nights.*

WALNUT TREE COTTAGE
Symonds Yat West, Near Ross-on-Wye HR9 6BN
0600 890828

We offer a high standard of accommodation in a friendly and relaxing atmosphere. Walnut Tree Cottage is set high on the River Wye and enjoys outstanding panoramic alpine-style views. There are excellent river and woodland walks. Above all the area offers the quiet timelessness of the English countryside at its finest and a true escape from the pressures and bustle of everyday life. All rooms are centrally heated; tea/coffee facilities; log fires in season. Please quote FHG when booking.

£ *Winter and Spring bargain breaks – 3 days half board in en suite room £82.00 per person.* ☐ *1 November 1990 to 31 May 1991 excluding Public Holidays. All year round rate of £59.00 per person for 2 days half board; £206.50 per person for 7 days half board.*

Herefordshire 67

WOODLEA HOTEL
Symonds Yat West
0600 890206

A comfortable Victorian licensed hotel in a tranquil woodland setting overlooking the Wye Rapids. The nine bedrooms are well appointed, with full central heating. Log fires ensure that public rooms are cosy and inviting in cooler weather, and there is a lounge bar in which guests can relax. Food is carefully selected and imaginatively cooked, with a choice of dishes. The hotel has an outdoor swimming pool. Every effort is made to ensure that guests enjoy all home comforts. AA listed; RAC acclaimed.

£ **£48.50-£57.50 per person for two nights dinner, bed and full English breakfast.** Weekdays all year, plus weekends from 28th October 1990 to 28th March 1991.

THE STEPPES COUNTRY HOUSE HOTEL
Ullingswick, Near Hereford HR1 3JG
0432 820424

The Steppes is a 17th century Country House Hotel and a listed building. It is renowned for its Cordon Bleu cuisine, high standards of comfort, and tranquil atmosphere. The accommodation consists of five double/twin bedrooms, all with private bathroom. The diningroom is probably one of the most charming rooms in the house, with its low beamed ceiling, inglenook fireplace, original floor, and pretty windows. The Steppes has been awarded a BTA commendation for nine consecutive years. Golf, fishing and horse riding are available locally.

£ **£68-£86 per person for two nights dinner, bed and breakfast.** All year.

THE CROFT COUNTRY HOUSE
Vowchurch, Hereford HR2 0QE
0981 550 226

The Croft is a charming country house where guests may be assured of the best of personal attention from resident owners. This is an ideal base for exploring the beautiful and unspoilt region of the Marches and border country. Individually-furnished bedrooms are well-appointed and all enjoy superb views. Traditional and imaginative British cooking is a feature on the menu, as are favourite Continental dishes, and much of the fruit and vegetables come from the Croft's own gardens.

£ **From £59 per person for 2 days dinner, bed and breakfast. Additional days pro rata.** From 1st October 1990 to 27th March 1991.

TUDOR GUEST HOUSE
The Post Office, Weobley HR4 8SA
0544 318201

The picturesque village of Weobley is situated 12 miles north of Hereford, in unspoilt countryside on the English/Welsh border. It is of great historic interest, with numerous Tudor properties, and lies on the "Black and White" Village Trail. Situated at the centre of the village, this small friendly Guest House, Grade II Listed, offers two double and two single rooms, all beautifully decorated with Laura Ashley soft furnishings. There are vanity units, tea and coffee making facilities; luxury guests' bathroom and separate WC; cosy TV lounge with log fires, tourist information, books and magazines. Full central heating. Licensed oak-beamed dining room serving good fresh food. Delightful cottage garden with patio sun-trap. Very high standards maintained.

£ **£45 (double occupancy) £50 (single room) per person for 2 nights' bed, breakfast and dinner.** All year except Christmas.

Hertfordshire

THE COTTAGE
71 Birchanger Lane, Bishop's Stortford CM23 5QF
0279 812349

Set in large, attractive gardens, the Cottage dates from the late 17th century and is a Grade II Listed building. It has been modernised to provide warm, comfortable yet characterful accommodation. AA Listed. All rooms have private shower, WC etc, colour TV, central heating and tea/coffee making facilities. Dining room and panelled sitting room, with log burning stove. Ample private parking. There are many pretty villages to visit; market towns such as Bishop's Stortford and Saffron Walden and fine country houses within easy reach. Cambridge 30 minutes, easy access to London.

£ *Terms on application.*

Other specialised

FHG PUBLICATIONS

* Recommended COUNTRY HOTELS OF BRITAIN £2.99

* Recommended WAYSIDE INNS OF BRITAIN £2.99

* PETS WELCOME! £2.50

* BED AND BREAKFAST IN BRITAIN £1.99

Published annually. Please add 50p postage (U.K. only)
when ordering from the publishers:

FHG PUBLICATIONS LTD
Abbey Mill Business Centre, Seedhill,
Paisley, Renfrewshire PA1 1JN

Isle of Wight

YELF'S HOTEL
Union Street, Ryde PO33 2LG
0983 64062 Fax: 0983 63937

[TA]

Yelf's is conveniently situated a short walk from the pier — ferry crossings can be booked if required. The comfortable bedrooms have private bathroom, colour TV, radio, telephone and tea/coffee facilities. RAC**. Children are especially welcome, and cots, highchairs and baby listening are available. Throughout the year there is a varied programme of entertainments for the whole family. Ryde, the island's largest resort, has a fine stretch of beach and a range of sports such as canoeing, golf, tennis, croquet and bowls.

[£] *Dinner, bed and breakfast from £35 per person per night, minimum 2 nights. All year. October – June: 5 nights for the price of 3 (must start Thursday or Sunday).*

HOLLIERS HOTEL
Old Village, Shanklin PO37 7NU
0983 862764

Holliers stands in the heart of the Old Village, looking out over thatched cottages, and is only a stroll from the beach and country. AA***. All bedrooms are en suite, with central heating, colour TV, tea/coffee facilities etc. Leisure amenities include swimming pools (indoor and outdoor), sauna, solarium, spa bath and pool table. The restaurant offers superb dining facilities, with a full choice at breakfast and dinner. For relaxation there is a residents' lounge, bar, wine bar and popular Village Inn with entertainment.

[£] *3-day spring and autumn breaks £108 per person for dinner, bed and breakfast. January–April and November, December (except Easter, Christmas and New Year).*

SUNNYHURST AND WIGHT HOUSE LUXURY APARTMENTS
Ventnor
0983 852259

[TA]

Wight House, sitting on Eastern Cliff, has uninterrupted, panoramic sea views. Most apartments have private balconies or patio doors. Telephone, library. **Sunnyhurst**, brand new for the 1990s, has superb sea views (except one), garden and barbecue area. Both have children's play area and car park. Quiet, but within minutes of beach, shopping centre, restaurants and coastal walks. Each flat is spacious and spotlessly clean (supervised by owners); 1/3 bedrooms, bathroom, lounge and kitchen with microwave, washing machine etc. For brochure contact Mr and Mrs J.O. Jones, Trewartha, Bath Road, Ventnor, Isle of Wight PO38 1JH (0983 852259).

[£] *Terms on application.*

Kent

VELINDRE HOTEL AND LEISURE COMPLEX
Western Esplanade, Broadstairs CT10 1TG
0843 61485

The Velindre has further extended its first-class restaurant, with a choice of à la carte, table d'hôte and grill menus. The leisure centre bar serves a bistro style menu and refreshments which can be enjoyed beside the indoor heated swimming pool. Superbly situated on cliffs overlooking the English Channel and within a short walk of the town centre and bays. The modern bedrooms have showers, radio, tea/coffee facilities; cots, high chairs, colour TV, free parking, baby listening intercom, table tennis and 8-ball pool are also available.

£ *2 nights accommodation with breakfast and dinner £90 per person; extra nights available on request when booking.*
🕒 *1st November to 30th April excluding Bank Holidays.*

BLERIOT'S GUEST HOUSE
185 Folkestone Road, Dover CT17 9SJ
0304 211394

A small, family-run guest house within easy reach of trains, bus station, Hoverport, town centre and docks. All rooms have tea-making facilities and washbasins, and are fully centrally heated. SEETB Listed. Off-road parking always available. Bleriot's makes an ideal base for visiting the many historic attractions in and around Dover, including Dover Castle, the Roman Painted House and the famous White Cliffs, or, if you prefer, a day trip to the Continent by ferry, hovercraft or jetfoil. For further details contact Mr and Mrs M. Casey.

£ *2 nights minimum £9.00 per person per night for bed and breakfast, singles £11.00.* 🕒 *October to April inclusive.*

ELMO GUEST HOUSE
120 Folkestone Road, Dover
0304 206236

A guest house specialising in short break holidays. Single, double, and family rooms are all available, with washbasin, shaver point, and television. There is also a colour television in the lounge/diner. Elmo Guest House is close to the stations, hoverport, and ferries. There are many local attractions in Dover, including the Castle and Roman painted house, while the Kentish countryside with its picturesque villages, historic Canterbury, and the Cinque Ports, is near at hand.

£ *From £20 to £25 per double room per night.* 🕒 *1 October to 30 April.*

WHITE CLIFFS HOTEL
Waterloo Crescent, Sea Front, Dover
0304 203633

A fully licensed hotel in a late 19th century terrace most conveniently situated on the sea front at Dover. The 54 bedrooms are well appointed, all comfortably furnished and with private bathrooms. AA***, RAC***. Many of the hotel's bedrooms enjoy fine views over Dover harbour and the English Channel. White Cliffs is superbly placed for Dover docks, Hoverport, and jetfoil for day trips to the Continent. Also ideal for visits to Dover Castle, day trips to Canterbury, and for touring the lovely Kentish countryside.

£ **£30 per person per night for two to five nights dinner, bed and breakfast.** ◷ *1 October 1990 to 31 May 1991.*

TUDOR COURT HOTEL
Hawkhurst
0580 752 312 Fax: 0580 753 966 Telex: 957565 TCH

This friendly country hotel is known for its excellent cuisine. There are extensive gardens with a children's adventure playground, croquet and clock golf. All rooms have radio and colour TV, direct-dial telephone, hairdryer, trouser press and tea/coffee making facilities. AA**, RAC**. There are plenty of activities to enjoy including tennis and nearby riding, golf and trout fishing. This is a good touring centre with Bodiam and Scotney Castles within easy reach. Camber Sands is a favourite with the children.

£ **From £106 per person with £5 daily à la carte allowance for any 2 nights dinner, bed and breakfast.** ◷ *All year, except Christmas.*

THE ROYAL OAK HOTEL
High Street, Sevenoaks TN14 5PG
0732 451109

The 17th century Royal Oak is ideally situated right in the heart of the "Garden of England", within easy access of London and the magnificent Kent countryside. AA***. The bedrooms, all with private bathrooms, are fitted to the highest standard with all modern facilities. The restaurant offers an imaginative combination of both nouvelle cuisine and English country cooking at its best. There is a friendly bar, popular with local residents, and a delightful conservatory. Hever Castle and Leeds Castle are just two of the many places of interest in the area.

£ **Dinner, bed and full English breakfast £42.50 per person per night (inc. VAT).** ◷ *1st April 1991 to 31st March 1992.*

THE SPA HOTEL
Mount Ephraim, Tunbridge Wells TN4 8XJ
0892 20331

Originally built in 1766, the Spa Hotel is ideally located for exploring the beautiful Kent countryside. RAC****. All bedrooms have private facilities. The Spa is family run and guests have free use of the leisure complex which includes sauna, heated pool, gymnasium, games room, beauty therapy and sun beds. Tennis, jogging track and children's playground are also available in the 14 acre grounds. Parking facilities for over 100 cars. The surrounding area contains a large number of historic houses, castles and gardens.

£ **£50-£55 per person per night dinner, bed and breakfast Friday, Saturday and Sunday plus any Bank Holiday. Minimum 2 nights.** ◷ *All year.*

IVYSIDE HOTEL
Sea Road, Westgate-on-Sea CT8 8SB
0843 31082

Set in its own gardens facing the golden sands of St. Mildred's Bay is this attractive hotel, ideal for families. AA**, RAC**. Each of the 68 bedrooms has TV, telephone, central heating, and private facilities. Interconnecting family suites are available, and the hotel provides babysitting, a playroom, parents' kitchen, and launderette. Other facilities include a games room, full size snooker table, indoor and outdoor pools, whirlpool, squash, sauna, solarium, and masseuse. Cabaret/dancing weekends. Featured on ITV's *Wish You Were Here*.

£ *From £26 per night for dinner, bed and breakfast. Children may stay free or at half or quarter price rates.*
September to May excluding Bank Holidays.

Lancashire

BARON HOTEL
296 North Promenade, Blackpool
0253 22729

Ideally situated on the Promenade overlooking the sea and within easy walking distance of the train station, theatres, Tower, pier, and Winter Gardens. The hotel's modern bedrooms all have television and tea making facilities, and all have shower and toilet en suite. A drink can be enjoyed with your meal, chosen from the excellent menu. Spacious sun lounge in which to relax. Large car park. Passenger lift.

£ *From £18 per person per day for bed and breakfast; from £20 for dinner, bed and breakfast.*

NEW OSBORNE PRIVATE HOTEL
9 Pleasant Street, North Shore, Blackpool FY1 2JA
0253 24578

Service with a smile is the keynote at this welcoming, family run hotel, only a minute's walk to the Promenade and close to the North Pier, town centre, and bus and train stations. The hotel has a residential licence, with a bar lounge where bar lunches are served. All rooms are well appointed, with colour television and tea and coffee making facilities and centrally heated, and there is a colour television lounge. Tasty home cooking is a speciality. Families are welcome. Proprietress Mrs B. Read.

£ *Bed and breakfast from £10.50 per night; bed, breakfast and evening meal from £12 per night. Any number of nights.* *All year.*

Kent/Lancashire 73

THE BIRCHLEY HOTEL
64 Holmfield Road, Blackpool FY2 9RT
0253 54174

The Birchley is a small but beautiful "no smoking" hotel, privately owned and managed by the resident proprietors. Situated in a very pleasant, select North Shore area, adjacent to Queen's Promenade. Come and enjoy a special weekend away, October to May, two nights from Friday with en suite accommodation, full English breakfast, evening dinner, and departing after a traditional Sunday luncheon. Want to know more? Just send a stamp, or telephone mentioning this guide and we will forward you our brochure with tariff and sample menus.

£ *2 nights Friday dinner to Sunday luncheon £50 per person. ✆ October 1990 to May 1991. Full week dinner, bed and breakfast £119 per person June to November 1991.*

THE PICKERINGS
Garstang Road, Catterall, Garstang PR3 0HA
0995 602133

[TA]

The Pickerings is a delightful country house situated in the small village of Catterall on the outskirts of the ancient market town of Garstang. An ideal base for touring the Fylde coast, Trough of Bowland, Lancashire and the Lake District. At The Pickerings the surroundings and service are for the discerning, with individually furnished lounges and bedrooms, hearty breakfasts and rich 5-course dinners. Two acres of well-tended gardens are available for relaxation, and nearby are several golf courses, nature trails and picnic sites. AA**

£ *From £80 per person for 2 nights dinner with champagne, bed and breakfast. ✆ Most weekends.*

SPREAD EAGLE HOTEL
Sawley, Near Clitheroe
0200 41202 or 41406

Why not treat yourself to a relaxing, carefree weekend in the country? Nestling on the banks of the River Ribble you will find the Spread Eagle Hotel and Restaurant. AA listed. Michelin. Most major credit cards accepted. Enjoy a weekend break in luxurious surroundings with full English breakfast served in your room. Dine on Friday and Saturday evenings at a reserved riverside table and leave after a leisurely lunch on Sunday.

£ *£89 per person for weekend break. ✆ All year.*

MYTTON FOLD FARM HOTEL
Whalley Road, Langho, Blackburn BB6 8AB
0254 240662

A warm Lancashire welcome awaits you at this privately owned and family-run hotel, situated at the gateway to the beautiful Ribble Valley. Mytton Fold offers peace and tranquillity, yet is within easy reach of the Lake District, the Yorkshire Dales and the holiday resorts of Blackpool and Morecambe. All the en suite bedrooms are furnished to a very high standard, with colour TV, radio/alarm, direct-dial telephone, tea/coffee facilities and hairdryer. The licensed restaurant specialises in home-cooked food, using fresh local produce wherever possible. Comfortable bar lounge and residents' lounge. AA/RAC***, Ashley Courtenay Recommended.

£ *Special weekend breaks £125 per couple for 2 nights (one of which must be a Saturday) bed, breakfast and dinner. ✆ All year except Christmas and New Year.*

Leicestershire

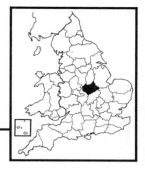

DENBIGH ARMS HOTEL AND RESTAURANT ♛ ♛ ♛ ♛ [TA]
High Street, Lutterworth LE17 4AD
0455 553537

Once a historic Georgian Coaching Inn, the Denbigh Arms has been stylishly redeveloped, retaining its traditional oak beams. All 34 bedrooms have private facilities together with all the comforts one would expect from a top 3 star hotel. AA/RAC ***, Michelin, Egon Ronay. The highly recommended restaurant offers a wide variety of excellent food. The historic small market town of Lutterworth has a famous 13th century church, where in 1374 the rector, John Wycliff, translated the Bible into English. This is an ideal central location for visiting many places of interest, located close to the M1 (Junction 20) and the M6 (Junction 1).
£ *Friday, Saturday, Sunday – any two nights £39.00 per person per night for dinner, room and breakfast.* ☐ *All year excluding Christmas week.*

THE WHIPPER-IN HOTEL ♛ ♛ ♛ ♛ [TA]
Market Place, Oakham LE15 6DT
0572 756971

This 17th century hotel sits in the market square of historic Oakham, only two miles from Rutland Water which provides opportunities for sailing, windsurfing and fishing. It is furnished throughout with antiques and old prints, and log fires burn in the lounges and bars when required. Imaginative English country cooking is a speciality of the restaurant, with an emphasis on game and fish. Bar meals are available, as well as locally brewed real ale. The bedrooms all have private bathrooms, remote-control TV and direct-dial telephone.
£ *Dinner, bed and English breakfast £85 per person for 2 night break, either Friday/Saturday or Saturday/Sunday.* ☐ *All year.*

NORMANTON PARK HOTEL ♛ ♛ ♛ ♛ [TA]
Rutland Water South Shore LE15 8RP
0780 720315 Fax: 0780 721086

Situated on the shores of Rutland Water, Normanton Park is a unique conservation award winning conversion of a Listed Georgian Coach House Stable. AA and RAC ***. Rutland Water, the largest man-made lake in Europe, provides 25 miles of walks and cycle tracks, and 3500 acres of water for sailing, windsurfing and fishing. Superb birdwatching area. The hotel has direct access to the lake and provides an ideal centre for lakeside activities. It is situated in the heart of England, with the historic towns of Stamford and Oakham nearby and the A1 only five minutes' drive.
£ *2 days fully inclusive £39 per person per night in a shared double/twin room.* ☐ *All year subject to availability.*

Leicestershire 75

Greater Manchester

RAMADA RENAISSANCE HOTEL
Blackfriars Street, Manchester M3 2EQ
061-835 2555 Fax: 061-835 3077

This four-star deluxe hotel is located in the heart of the city, near main shops, theatres and Granada Studio tours. The 205 guest rooms have either one kingsize bed or two double beds, lounge area, large bathroom and colour TV with satellite channels. The Deansgate Restaurant and bar offer a wide selection of snacks and international dishes. Special interest weekends include: Murder Mystery, Art Lovers, Psychic, Healthy Living, Ballroom Dancing, Golf, Blackpool Lights and Mill Shops, Wine and Gourmet, Aintree and Theatre Breaks.

£ *Special weekend rates for 2 persons sharing a room; £50 per night (one night), £45 per night (2 nights), £40 per night (3 nights).* ☐ *October 1990–May 1991 subject to availability.*

EXPLANATION OF SYMBOLS

TA	Travel Agency Commission
♛	Number of Crowns
⚷	Number of Keys
🐕	Pets Welcome
🐎	Reductions for Children
♿	Suitable for Disabled
🌲	Christmas Breaks

The symbols are arranged in the
same order throughout the book so that
looking down each page will give a quick comparison.

76 *Greater Manchester*

Merseyside

STUTELEA HOTEL & LEISURE CLUB
Alexandra Road, Southport PR9 0NB
0704 544220

A charming hotel offering fine hospitality and excellent cuisine. AA**, RAC**. The 18 bedrooms are well appointed, and all have private bathroom. Lift. For those who prefer greater privacy Stutelea also offers nine apartments. There are superb leisure facilities, with an indoor heated pool, jacuzzi, sauna, solarium and gym, games room, lounge with library, two licensed bars, and restaurant where the Grand Victorian breakfast is served until noon on Sunday. Good shopping and golf.

£ *2 nights dinner, bed and breakfast per person £67 (October 1990–June 1991), £69 (July and August 1991).* Except Christmas, Bank Holidays and Aintree Grand National Weekend.

THE GILTON HOTEL
7 Leicester Street, Southport
0704 530646

A small family hotel situated close to the Promenade and Lord Street's famous shopping area. All bedrooms have tea making facilities, and some are en suite. The Gilton has a restaurant and bar with pool table and games room. Botanical gardens, a swimming pool, marine lake, and zoo are all in the Southport area and are within easy reach of the hotel, and five championship golf courses lie within five miles.

£ *£18 per person for bed and breakfast. Evening Meal £7.50. Extra nights pro rata.* 1 October to 30 April excluding Christmas. Special rates for four-day Christmas house party.

HOLIDAY ACCOMMODATION
Classification Schemes in England, Scotland and Wales

The National Tourist Boards for England, Scotland and Wales have agreed a common 'Crown Classification' scheme for **serviced (Board)** accommodation. All establishments are inspected regularly and are given a classification indicating their level of facilities and services.

There are six grades ranging from 'Listed' to 'Five Crowns'. The higher the classification, the more facilities and services offered. Crown classification is a measure of *facilities* not *quality*. A common quality grading scheme grades the quality of establishments as 'Approved', 'Commended' or 'Highly Commended' according to the accommodation, welcome and service they provide.

For **Self-Catering**, holiday homes in England are awarded 'Keys' after inspection and can also be 'Approved', 'Commended' or 'Highly Commended' according to the facilities available. In Scotland the Crown scheme includes self-catering accommodation and Wales also has a voluntary inspection scheme for self-catering grading from '1 (Standard)' to '5 (Excellent)'.

Caravan and Camping Parks can participate in the British Holiday Parks grading scheme from 'Approved' (✓) to 'Excellent' (✓✓✓✓). In addition, each National Tourist Board has an annual award for high-quality caravan accommodation: in England – Rose Awards; in Scotland – Thistle Commendations; in Wales – Dragon Awards.

When advertisers supply us with the information, FHG Publications show Crowns and other awards or gradings, including AA, RAC, Egon Ronay etc. We also award a small number of Farm Holiday Guide Diplomas every year, based on readers' recommendations.

Merseyside 77

Norfolk

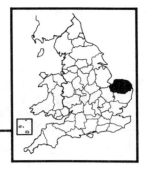

THE KING'S HEAD HOTEL
Dereham NR19 1AD
0362 693842 Fax: 0362 693776

The King's Head is a 17th century hotel, thoroughly modernised to meet today's high requirements, and conveniently situated within easy reach of the Norfolk Broads and Norwich. This essentially family concern maintains high standards of comfort, courteous service and good English cooking. All bedrooms are centrally heated, with colour TV and tea/coffee making facilities, and most have private bathrooms or showers. The attractive restaurant offers an intimate setting for the enjoyment of carefully prepared food; bar meals served daily. AA/RAC**. Les Routiers.
£ *Two persons sharing a room: dinner, bed and breakfast £30 per person (dinner to value of £10).*

CROSSKEYS RIVERSIDE HOTEL
Hilgay, Downham Market PE38 0LN
0366 387777

Approved

A small country hotel beside the tranquil River Wissey, at the gateway to West Norfolk. Formerly a coaching inn, it has been carefully renovated to retain its original character. The dining room with oak beams and inglenook fireplace offers à la carte, table d'hôte and vegetarian menus, complemented by a selection from the rustic bar. Bedrooms with en suite bathrooms have colour TV, tea/coffee facilities; three have four-poster beds. Family room available. The large riverside garden offers boating and fishing, or is ideal for just relaxing. AA Listed, RAC Highly Acclaimed.
£ *Special breaks for two: 2 nights dinner, bed and breakfast £49.75 per person.* ☐ *1st October 1990 to 31st March 1991; £54.25 from 1st April 1991.*

INGLENEUK LODGE
Hopton Road, Garboldisham, Diss IP22 2RQ
095-381 541

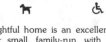

Connie and Doug Atkins' delightful home is an excellent centre for touring East Anglia: small, family-run, with a homely atmosphere and 11 acres of grounds and woodland. Guestaccom, RAC Highly Acclaimed. Its quiet rural situation with a small stream offers the opportunity to see lots of wildlife. Most rooms have en suite shower or bath, and all have remote control colour TV, hot drinks facilities, telephone, central heating and electric blankets for winter breaks. There is a licensed bar/lounge and a spacious car park.
£ *Dinner, bed and breakfast en suite sharing £56 per person for 2 nights. Room with washbasin only, £46.* ☐ *Until Easter 1991.*

THE OLD RECTORY
Gissing, Diss IP22 3XB
037977 575 Fax: 037977 4427

This delightful Victorian house stands in substantial grounds five miles north of Diss and central for touring East Anglia. Beautifully furnished and decorated, it is a haven of peace, comfort and elegance. All bedrooms have en suite or private bathrooms. Every effort has been made to ensure a memorable stay — tea and coffee making facilities, colour television, fresh flowers and many other thoughtful extras. Candlelit dinner is available by prior arrangement. Guests may use the covered heated swimming pool between May and October. Good Room Award — Guestaccom.

[£] *Bed and breakfast £20-£22 per person per night (based on double occupancy). 4-course dinner £14. Reduced rates available for mid-week breaks (bed and breakfast only).*

THE BLAKENEY HOTEL
Blakeney, Holt
0263 740797

Overlooking National Trust Harbour, and in its own gardens, the Blakeney has 50 bedrooms, all with private bathroom, colour TV and telephone. Amenities include a heated indoor swimming pool, saunas, hair salon, games room, and lounges. Conference rooms. Ample parking. À la carte and table d'hôte dinners and lunches in the restaurant. AA***, RAC***. Excellent for relaxing, sailing, walking, cycling, golfing, birdwatching, and viewing historic places including Sandringham and the Norfolk villages and countryside.

[£] *From £48 per person per day according to season.*
All year except Bank Holiday Weekends.

BARNHAM BROOM HOTEL
CONFERENCE AND LEISURE CENTRE
Norwich NR9 4DD
060-545 393 Fax: 060545 8224

Situated 8 miles west of Norwich and set in 250 acres, the complex incorporates two 18 hole golf courses, squash/tennis courts, swimming pool, fitness gym, sauna, solarium and beautician. The hotel offers 52 en suite bedrooms with colour television, radio and telephone. This hotel, conference and leisure centre is ideal for lovers of good food, assiduous service, and contemporary comforts. AA*** Best Western Worldwide Hotels member.

[£] *Sunday night specials from £40 per person. Getaway breaks from £96, golfing getaways from £124.*
All year except Christmas and New Year when special package rates apply.

GOLF GUIDE
WHERE TO PLAY
AND
WHERE TO STAY
PGA

Available from most bookshops, the 1991 edition of THE GOLF GUIDE covers details of every UK golf course – well over 2000 entries – for holiday or business golf. Hundreds of hotel entries offer convenient accommodation, accompanying details of the courses – the 'pro', par score, length etc.

Old Thorns Golf Course & Hotel, Hampshire, features on the front cover with golfing editorial from the Professional Golfers' Association who also endorse the guide.

£5.99 from bookshops or £6.50 including postage from FHG Publications, Abbey Mill Business Centre, Paisley PA1 1JN.

CUMBERLAND HOTEL
212-214 Thorpe Road, Norwich NR1 1TJ
0603 34550/34560 Fax: 0603 33355

A family run hotel offering fine personal and friendly service and set in its own grounds with ample parking for guests. The delightful candlelit Veranda Restaurant offers a variety of succulent dishes, and guests can relax in the elegant lounge bar and residents' television lounge. All bedrooms are well equipped, with colour TV and tea and coffee making facilities. Direct dial telephones and radio alarms in all rooms. Executive rooms available. The hotel is situated within minutes of the 'fine city' of Norwich, and allows easy access to Broads and coast.

[£] *From £47.00 per person for two nights dinner, bed and breakfast. Extra nights from £22.00.* [] *All year.*

THE GARDEN HOUSE HOTEL
Salhouse Road, Rackheath, Norwich NR13 6AA
0603 720007

Superb food, comfortable accommodation, a relaxed informal atmosphere and lovely surroundings — the Garden House recipe for a really enjoyable holiday. Ideally situated for the city of Norwich, the Norfolk Broads and the coast, with adequate parking, the hotel boasts a restaurant renowned in the area for its classic English cooking, specialising in fresh local vegetables and game and shellfish in season. All rooms have telephone, colour TV and beverage making facilities. Most rooms en suite. Large lounge with bar, 2 dining rooms, one of which overlooks the lovely gardens.

[£] *2 nights dinner, bed and breakfast £60 per person.*

ABBEY HOTEL
10 Church Street, Wymondham NR18 0PH
0953 602148 Fax: 0953 606247

The tour of Norfolk takes us to the quiet old market town of Wymondham, where this attractive hotel stands opposite the 12th century abbey. Recent renovations have exposed old beams in several of the bedrooms, and modern amenities have been carefully blended with the time-honoured appeal of the building. All the handsomely decorated bedrooms are en suite, and have television, radio and tea/coffee making facilities. AA**. There is a comfortable lounge, and the Cardinal Restaurant and Pilgrims Bar are available for wining and dining. Yesterday's charm — today's comfort. A Best Western Hotel.

[£] *Getaway Breaks from £76.*

PUBLISHER'S NOTE

While every effort is made to ensure accuracy, we regret that FHG Publications cannot accept responsibility for errors, omissions or misrepresentation in our entries or any consequences thereof. Prices in particular should be checked because we go to press early. We will follow up complaints but cannot act as arbiters or agents for either party.

Northumberland

BISHOPFIELD COUNTRY HOUSE HOTEL
Allendale, Hexham NE47 9EJ
0434 683248 Fax: 0434 683830

This fine eighteenth century country house hotel stands in beautiful countryside, and offers peace, tranquillity and relaxation in charming surroundings. Proprietors Keith and Kathy Fairless's insistence on the very highest standards of accommodation and cuisine have earned Bishopfield an excellent reputation for its French to English cooking, served in the attractive dining room. All bedrooms have full central heating, private facilities and colour television. Fishing available nearby. AA and RAC**.

£ *Bed and breakfast from £22 per person per night.*
November 1990 – end May 1991.

MARINE HOUSE PRIVATE HOTEL
1 Marine Road, Alnmouth NE66 2RW
0665 830349

This 200-year-old stone house, once a granary, is situated on the edge of the village golf links overlooking beautiful beaches. It has been recently modernised, but retains its original charm. There are 10 comfortable bedrooms, all en suite, and a cocktail bar, games room and spacious TV lounge with log fire. Local leisure activities include fishing, sea angling, pony trekking and golf (venues can be booked). Alnmouth is ideally situated for exploring the magnificent Northumberland coastline.

£ *£57 per person for 2 nights dinner, bed and breakfast; extra nights pro rata. 1st October to 30th November 1990; 1st February to 30th April 1991.*

BREAMISH COUNTRY HOUSE HOTEL
Powburn, Alnwick NE66 4LL
066-578 266

Breamish House is a charming, Georgian style country house hotel set in five acres overlooking the Cheviots. The hotel is peaceful and relaxing with friendly service. Breamish offers 10 bedrooms, all with private facilities, colour television, radio, telephone and tea/coffee making facilities. In the evenings, the diningroom is candle lit and guests can enjoy a five-course meal made from excellent ingredients. Two lounges with log fires are also a feature of Breamish Hotel.

£ *Full details on request.*

DUNSTANBURGH CASTLE HOTEL
Embleton, Near Alnwick NE66 3UN
0665 76203

Situated in the centre of a quiet unspoilt village, 10 minutes' walk from magnificent clean, sandy beaches and National Trust coastline. Bedrooms are comfortable and well-equipped, and most are en suite and have colour TV. A choice of menu is offered, featuring a varied selection of home-cooked dishes using the best of local produce. For relaxation there are comfortable lounges with open fires, and a cosy cocktail bar. We are a long-established business, with many revisits and recommendations from our guests.

£ *£25 per person per day for dinner, bed and breakfast — 3 nights minimum.* ⌧ *Various dates throughout the year.*

VALLUM LODGE HOTEL
Military Road, Twice Brewed, Near Bardon Mill NE47 7AN
0434 344248

Commended

Situated in open countryside close by Hadrian's Wall in Northumberland National Park, this delightful, quiet and peaceful hotel offers every comfort. AA*. All seven ground floor rooms have washbasins and teamakers. Residents' bar, lounge with TV, large garden. Excellent freshly prepared food using local produce. Convenient for all Roman sites and country houses; excellent walking area. Large car park. A warm and friendly welcome awaits you.

£ *Dinner, bed and breakfast £48 per person for 2 nights; £72 for 3 nights; extra nights £24. Private facilities extra.* ⌧ *1 March to mid-June, mid-September to 30 November.*

RIVERDALE HALL HOTEL & RESTAURANT
Bellingham
0434 220254

Victorian country house hotel with RAC Merit awarded restaurant. All bedrooms have bath and shower, television, telephone and tea/coffee making facilities. Riverdale Hall is the nearest hotel to the beautiful Kielder Water and Forest and is close to the Pennine Way, National Trust walks and Hadrian's Wall. This hotel is popular with the sporting enthusiast and has its own indoor swimming pool, games room, sauna, cricket field, and salmon and trout river, with a golf course opposite.

£ *From £62 in winter to £78 in summer for two night break with dinner, en suite room and breakfast. Extra nights pro rata.* ⌧ *All year.*

KNOWESGATE HOTEL
Kirkwhelpington NE19 2SH
0830 40261

This small, stone-built, family-run hotel is situated on the edge of the National Park. All rooms have private bathrooms, colour TV and tea-makers. Some ground floor rooms. Ideal for walking and touring Northumberland, Scottish Borders and local National Trust properties. AA**.

£ *Terms on application.*

Oxfordshire

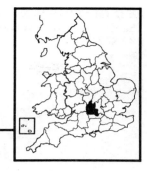

ABINGDON LODGE HOTEL
Marcham Road, Abingdon OX14 1TZ
0235 553456 Telex 837750

This privately owned and managed hotel, opened in June 1986, is seven miles from Oxford and ideally placed, on the junction of the A34/415, for visiting Blenheim Palace and touring the Cotswolds. AA***, RAC*** recommended. The 63 bedrooms have private facilities, radio, television with in-house movies, trouser press, self-controlled heating, hospitality tray and direct dial telephone. There is ample parking for guests at the Lodge.

£ *£70 per person for two nights, dinner, bed and breakfast. Extra night pro rata. Available Friday night to Sunday night inclusive and every night during August plus Easter and Bank Holidays.* ⌂ *All year.*

KING'S HEAD INN & RESTAURANT
The Green, Bledington, Near Kingham OX7 6HD
060-871 365

A 15th century coaching inn standing on a beautiful Cotswolds village green. Egon Ronay, Michelin, Derek Johansen, AA. The King's Head has an authentic, beamed interior with inglenook fireplace. All bedrooms are en suite, with colour TV, telephone and tea and coffee making facilities. An à la carte menu is served in the restaurant six nights a week, and bar meals are also available. The King's Head has a garden room and garden. Set as it is in the heart of the Cotswolds, it is ideal for touring or for day visits to Stratford, Cheltenham, Stow-on-the-Wold and Bourton-on-the-Water.

£ *£85 for two nights bed and breakfast for two people; £125 for three nights.* ⌂ *31 October 1990 to 31 March 1991.*

HOLCOMBE HOTEL
Deddington OX5 4SL
0869 38274

This charming 17th century family run hotel offers the perfect stay for anyone seeking a rural setting in the beautiful Cotswold countryside. The ambience of the restaurant and its cuisine are particular features with emphasis on relaxation and warm, friendly service. We are ideally located to visit Broughton Castle, Woodstock and Blenheim Palace, Warwick and Stratford-upon-Avon. The hotel offers 17 bedrooms, all en suite with all modern amenities. AA**; featured in Ashley Courtenay and Michelin.

£ ⌂ *Full details on request.*

OLD GEORGE INN
The Greens, Leafield OX8 5NP
099-387 288

This charming village inn is situated on the green in the lovely Cotswold village of Leafield. On the edge of Wychwood Forest, Blenheim Palace and Woodstock are only 8 miles away; Burford and the Wild Life Park are 5 miles away. All bedrooms have TV. Good food is served in the restaurant, and bar snacks are also available. Les Routiers.

£ *From £22 single, £32 double with en suite facilities. Reductions for longer stays.*

HILLBOROUGH HOTEL AND RESTAURANT
The Green, Milton-Under-Wychwood OX7 6JH
0993 830501

Commended

This is a small, luxurious Victorian hotel, facing the village green. AA, RAC. AA Best Newcomer 1989. All rooms have private bathroom, colour TV, direct-dial telephones and tea/coffee making facilities. Hillborough Hotel offers a cosy restaurant and bar with open fires and a selection of good food and wine. The conservatory lounge faces onto the gardens and croquet lawn. Private parking. Ideal base to visit the medieval town of Burford, with Oxford, Stratford-on-Avon and market towns within easy reach. Fishing can be arranged locally.

£ *£32 per person per night for dinner, bed and breakfast, two night minimum.* ⌂ *February-December.*

THE OLD SWAN AND MILL
Minster Lovell OX8 5RN
0993 774441

[TA]

Tucked away in the picturesque Cotswold village of Minster Lovell, The Old Swan and Mill retains its historic charm, while providing the finest in today's comforts and service. The 18 en suite bedrooms all have colour TV and telephone. The charming public lounges are comfortable and relaxing. In the beamed, candlelit restaurant imaginative menus are prepared from fresh produce; bar snacks are also available at lunchtimes. Ideally situated for exploring the Cotswolds, Oxford, Cheltenham and many other places of interest. Tennis, fishing, punting, putting and croquet all available by the banks of the river which flows through the grounds. AA***, Egon Ronay.

£ *Any two nights Friday/Saturday/Sunday £280-£310 twin/double, £192-£218 single for dinner, bed and breakfast. 4-poster suite £344-£388.* ⌂ *All year.*

WESTWOOD COUNTRY HOTEL
Hinksey Hill Top, Oxford OX1 5BG
0865 735408 Fax: 0865 736536

A family-run hotel with 26 bedrooms, all with private facilities, radio, intercom, colour TV, hairdryer, video and tea/coffee making facilities. Three acres of garden and woodland. Excellent food. Log fires in cold weather. Intimate bar. For hotel guests sauna, jacuzzi and mini-gym available. Awarded Hotel of the Year 1987 (Booker Foods), AA Listed, RAC**, Michelin.

£ *From £60 for double room, from £45 for single room (for bed and full English breakfast in en suite room).*

THE WELL HOUSE
High Street, Watlington OX9 5PY
049-161 3333

The Well House is delightfully situated at the foot of the Chiltern Hills in the pretty conservation village of Watlington only two miles from the M40. Michelin, Relais Routiers. It has nine bedrooms with private facilities. There is also a first-class restaurant. Squash and tennis may be arranged. This is an ideal centre for touring the beautiful Cotswolds and Chilterns, with walks over National Trust land, Blenheim, Oxford, and Stonor Park all nearby.

£ **£70-£80 per person for two nights dinner, bed and breakfast; £100-£110 for three nights. Prices based on two persons sharing en suite room, and include VAT.** ⌂ *All year.*

Shropshire

COURT FARM
Gretton, Church Stretton SY6 7HU
06943 219

Commended

Large, stone Tudor farmhouse on 325-acre working farm. Situated in very rural surroundings just outside village of Cardington and within easy distance of most interesting places in Shropshire. Ideal situation for sightseeing, walking and relaxing. RAC Acclaimed. Three double rooms — one en suite and two with washbasins; separate lounge and dining-room. Tea and coffee making facilities. Colour television and log fires. High quality cuisine. NON SMOKING HOUSEHOLD. RAC comment: "A place worth seeking".

£ *Bed, breakfast and dinner from £23 per person per night. Bed and breakfast only from £15.* ⌂ *February to November.*

THE REDFERN HOTEL
Cleobury Mortimer DY14 8AA
0299 270395

Standing in the lovely old market town of Cleobury Mortimer is this fine hotel, perfect for a getaway break in this most interesting area. Ironbridge Industrial Museum is just 20 miles away, and Acton Scott Farm Museum will take visitors back to the days of the Shire horse. Severn Valley Railway is also near at hand. Visitors can return after a hard day's sightseeing to good food, fine wines, and friendly service. All the comfortable rooms have private bathrooms, TV with inhouse video, telephone, hot drinks facilities, and several thoughtful extras.

£ **£64 per person for two nights dinner, bed and breakfast.** ⌂ *All year except Christmas and New Year.*

STREFFORD HALL
Strefford, Craven Arms SY7 8DE
0588 672383

Guests are assured of a warm welcome at this spacious Victorian farmhouse on a working farm keeping cattle and sheep and growing corn. The Hall stands in a large garden and offers outstanding views of the Wenlock Edge and Long Mynd hills. Just off A49, 5 miles south of Church Stretton. AA Listed. Accommodation is in one double, one family and one twin bedroom, all with washbasins and shaver points. Tea/coffee facilities. Guests' bathroom, two toilets; lounge with colour TV; diningroom. Non-smokers preferred.
£ *Bed and breakfast from £12.50, evening meal £7.50. Reductions for 3 nights or more.* ⧖ *February to end November.*

THE HUNDRED HOUSE HOTEL
Bridgnorth Road, Norton, Near Telford TF11 9EE
095-271 353 Fax: 095-271 355

Character, charm and a warm atmosphere combine in this award-winning country inn, only three-quarters of an hour from Birmingham, and ideal for exploring the natural beauty of the Shropshire countryside. All en suite bedrooms have colour TV, radio, direct-dial telephone and tea/coffee facilities; some with antique half-tester beds and swings. The hotel has a growing reputation for varied and interesting menus, all freshly prepared. A range of traditional beers is served in the bar, which features beamed ceilings and oak panelling. AA**, RAC***, Merit Award, Les Routiers, Egon Ronay, 1989 "Best Inn in Shropshire" (Consumers Association).
£ *Minimum 2 days, £85 per night for two persons sharing room, inclusive of full meal in dining room. £10 supplement for Honeymoon Suite.* ⧖ *All year.*

TELFORD HOTEL GOLF & COUNTRY CLUB
Great Hay, Sutton Hill, Telford TF7 4DT
0952 585642 Telex: 35481 Fax: 0952 586602

Standing in a much envied position overlooking the truly magnificent and historic Ironbridge Gorge, the Telford is encompassed by both its own nine and 18 hole golf courses. AA***. In addition to this, it boasts indoor facilities such as swimming pool, sauna, snooker tables and squash court. For the less energetic, the 58 en suite bedrooms are equipped with TV, direct dial telephone and tea/coffee making facilities. For relaxation, there are two bars and a restaurant offering a variety of excellent cuisine.
£ *£83 per person sharing a twin bedded room for two nights, exclusive of golf, £112 inclusive of golf. Single supplement of £7.50 per night.* ⧖ *All year.*

EXPLANATION OF SYMBOLS

TA	Travel Agency Commission
♛	Number of Crowns
⚿	Number of Keys
🐕	Pets Welcome
⧖	Reductions for Children
♿	Suitable for Disabled
🎄	Christmas Breaks

86 *Shropshire*

Somerset

SHRUB FARM COUNTRY HOUSE HOTEL
Burton Row, Brent Knoll TA9 4BX
0278 760479

500-year-old farmhouse of immense character set in four acres of beautiful countryside. This family-run hotel is ideal for your short break, main holiday or overnight stop. ETB. WCTB. The Hotel is two miles from the sea, yet close to the Mendip Hills, so ideal for touring Somerset and Avon. It is fully licensed, with central heating and a log fire burns on chillier evenings. All rooms en suite, with colour TV, tea/coffee facilities, trouser press, hairdryer and direct-dial telephone. Close to Exit 22 of M5.

£ *2 nights £50 per person, 3 nights £70, 7 nights £145.*
🗓 *All year except Christmas, Bank Holidays and high season.*

WOODLANDS HOTEL
Hill Lane, Brent Knoll TA9 4DF
0278 760232

 TA

Nestling in its own wooded grounds and with splendid views across open country to the Quantock Hills, Woodlands offers a real country house atmosphere, together with every modern facility to ensure guests' comfort. Ground floor rooms available. Resident owners Mr and Mrs Gibson take particular pride in the very high standard of home cooking and in the varied menus available in the dining room, and are happy to cater for special diets by arrangement. There are secluded gardens and a heated swimming pool. Many places of interest in the area.

£ *Bed and breakfast from £13.50 per night.* 🗓 *All year.*

FRIARN COURT HOTEL
37 St. Mary Street, Bridgwater TA6 3LX
0278 452859 Fax: 0278 452988

   TA

Meet new people and make new friends while discovering the attractions of Somerset. Whatever your interest — whether it is exploring churches or gardens, cathedrals or stately homes, local crafts or museums, walking, fishing, golf or wildlife, you will find Somerset a treasure trove of pleasurable activities. Send now for our selection of carefully planned weekend break packages and look forward to spending a luxurious, sociable and interesting weekend relaxing with us in the heart of Somerset.

£ *Terms on request.*

THE WHITE HART
Fore Street, Castle Cary BA7 7BQ
0963 50255

This beautifully renovated old coaching inn dates back to the seventeenth century and today, under its welcoming hosts, Charlie and Fiona Anderson, specialises in good home cooking. In such a convivial atmosphere relaxation comes easily, with unspoilt countryside to walk and enjoy. Castle Cary is ideally placed for visits to numerous places of geographic and historic interest, and the coast is within an hour's drive. The inn has very comfortably appointed accommodation, and the terms represent excellent value for money.

£ *Bed and breakfast from £15 per person single, £26 double, with reductions for stays of 5 days or more.*

BROADVIEW
East Street, Crewkerne TA18 7AG (Dorset Border)
0460 73424

Commended for quality. Winner of Good Room Award. Secluded, really comfortable Colonial Bungalow, traditionally furnished, with a wonderfully relaxing atmosphere. Set in an acre of feature gardens including fish ponds and many interesting shrubs and trees. Three carefully furnished and decorated en suite rooms, each with easy chairs, remote control colour television, tea/coffee facilities and luxury bath/shower, basin and toilet. Fully controllable central heating. Situated in an area of outstanding natural beauty. So much to see and do. List provided of over 50 places to visit.

£ *Bed and full English breakfast £14.50; substantial quality home-cooked dinner £8.50. Open all year.*

THE OLD PARSONAGE
Barn Street, Crewkerne TA18 8BP
0460 73516

The Old Parsonage was originally, as the name suggests, the Parsonage to Crewkerne's famous 15th century church. Indeed, a secret tunnel to the church is rumoured to exist. The building is partly 15th and 18th century, and is set in its own gardens in the heart of this country town. The hotel, with its welcoming open fires, has ten bedrooms, all en suite, with TV and telephones. Located near many beautiful gardens and National Trust properties, 18 miles from the coast. Ballooning breaks and Gardeners' breaks a speciality.

£ *£40 per person per night for dinner, bed and breakfast. Minimum stay two nights. All year.*

EXMOOR HOUSE HOTEL
West Street, Dunster TA24 6SN
0643 821268

An attractive Georgian building set in the charming village of Dunster. AA and RAC**, Michelin. The rooms are bright and sunny in summer and centrally heated in winter. Bedrooms are en suite, with TV, radio and tea/coffee making facilities. Farm-fresh West Country produce is used to prepare varied and 'different' menus, plus an extensive wine list. The proprietors emphasise the home comforts, good food, and personal attention of a small hotel in a relaxed and informal atmosphere. Ideal for Exmoor and NT properties. An exclusively 'no smoking' hotel.

£ *£64-£70 for two nights dinner, bed and breakfast. Extra nights pro rata. Reductions for 5 nights or more. Prices according to season. February to November.*

BATCH FARM COUNTRY HOTEL
Lympsham, Near Weston-super-Mare BS24 0EX
0934-750 371

An air of old world charm pervades Batch Farm Country Hotel, lending atmosphere to the modern accommodation. Guests are welcome here all year except Christmas, and the ten bedrooms, all en suite, are comfortably fitted. Colour television and tea/coffee making facilities in all rooms. For guests' relaxation, there is a fully licensed lounge bar and three lounges. Traditional home cooking is served using local produce on a varied menu. Ample parking in own grounds. AA**, RAC, Egon Ronay and Ashley Courtenay Recommended. Most cards accepted.

£ **£32 per person per night for dinner, bed and breakfast.**

THE GEORGE INN AT NUNNEY
Church Street, Nunney, Near Frome BA11 4LW
037-384 458/565

Set in the picturesque village of Nunney, opposite the moated Norman castle, the George is a recommended touring headquarters. Places of interest include Longleat, Stourhead lake and gardens, the cathedral city of Wells and Cheddar caves. The inn has many attractions on its own account, especially the excellent food, served lunchtimes and evenings together with real ale. Comfortable accommodation is available in well-appointed rooms, almost all en suite. Pets welcome by arrangement. AA**, Egon Ronay.

£ **Bargain breaks available throughout the year from £30 per person per night for dinner, bed and breakfast.**

RUMWELL MANOR HOTEL
Rumwell, Taunton TA4 1EL
0823 461902

This elegant Georgian house is set in five acres of gardens, with panoramic views across the rolling Somerset pastures in the picturesque Vale of Taunton Deane. You will find us well placed for exploring the West Country and as a haven in which to relax. All the rooms are spacious, with full facilities, and some have four-poster beds. AA and RAC***. Our candlelit restaurant offers a choice from the table d'hôte menu which changes nightly, or full à la carte, in addition to a fine selection of wines.

£ **£79-£89 per person for any two nights dinner, bed and full English breakfast.** ☐ **Open all year.**

CHARLTON HOUSE HOTEL AND RESTAURANT
Charlton Road, Shepton Mallet BA4 4PR
0749 342008

This 17th century country house hotel is set amidst six acres of picturesque gardens and is ideally situated for touring. Leisure facilities include indoor heated swimming pool, sauna and tennis court. The 19 bedrooms are all en suite and have TV, direct dial telephone and tea/coffee making facilities. Some have four poster beds. RAC***. Ashley Courtenay recommended. The renowned restaurant uses only the finest of ingredients and there is an extensive wine list as well as a comfortable bar/lounge.

£ **From £95 to £110 dinner, bed and breakfast for two people sharing a double room. Two nights minimum.**
☐ **All year except for Bath and West Show Week.**

PENSCOT FARMHOUSE HOTEL
Shipham BS25 1TW
093-484 2659

This 16th century old world hotel, lying at the foot of the Mendips, manages to combine friendly informality with the highest standards of comfort and service. AA*, RAC*. Penscot enjoys a reputation for good, home cooked food chosen from its à la carte restaurant menu, or its table d'hôte guests' menu, served in the relaxed diningroom. Extensive and attractive grounds provide a charming setting, with a sunken rose garden. Ideal for touring the Somerset countryside.

£ *From £58 for two night break of dinner, bed and breakfast. Three nights from £85. Supplement for en suite room. Longer stays available.* ⌕ February to November excluding Bank Holidays.

HORSINGTON HOUSE HOTEL
Horsington, Templecombe BA8 0EG
0963 70721

A superb Georgian style hotel set in seven acres of gardens. AA**, RAC***. Bedrooms are en suite and elegantly furnished, all with colour TV, direct dial telephone, tea and coffee making facilities, and welcome pack with complementary newspaper. There are superb table d'hôte and gourmet menus, with several imaginative specialities. Tennis, croquet, and putting are all available in the grounds, and there is a play area for children. An ideal base for touring Somerset, Wiltshire, and Dorset.

£ *£37.50 per person per night dinner, bed and breakfast when sharing twin/double room. Minimum 2 nights.* ⌕ *Until end March 1991.*

YEW TREE COUNTRY HOUSE
Sand, Wedmore
0934 712520

This delightful 18th century country house, set in two acres of grounds, has been sympathetically restored to retain its fine period features. Accommodation is of a high standard, with en suite facilities, colour TV and tea/coffee making equipment. RAC Acclaimed. We have earned a reputation for excellent food, complemented by a good range of wines. This is an ideal area for country and field sports and there are many places of interest to visit nearby. Wells, Glastonbury and Cheddar are within easy reach, and the Georgian village of Wedmore is one mile away.

£ *£58 per person for 2 nights dinner, bed and breakfast.* ⌕ *Until Easter, but excluding Christmas and New Year.*

FAIRFIELD HOUSE HOTEL
51 Long Street, Williton TA4 4QY
0984 32636

Fairfield is a small licensed hotel which manages to combine 17th century charm with modern comfort. RAC, Michelin, Taste of Somerset, Good Food Guide. Bedrooms are tastefully furnished and equipped with tea/coffee making facilities, clock radios and private bath/shower rooms. Breakfast and dinner are taken in the hotel's Quantock Restaurant where the chef/proprietor offers a choice of dishes, all home cooked, using fresh local produce, home-baked rolls, imaginative sweets and always fresh vegetables. There is local cider, beer and even Somerset wine in the bar. An ideal base for exploring the Quantock Hills and Exmoor.

£ *3-day break dinner, bed and breakfast £85 per person, extra nights £28.* ⌕ *Easter to October inclusive.*

90 *Somerset*

Staffordshire

THE THREE HORSESHOES INN
Blackshaw Moor, Leek ST13 8TW
053-834 296

This family-run inn is situated on the A53, just 7 miles from Buxton and 20 minutes' drive from Alton Towers, with breathtaking views of the Staffordshire moorlands. The stone walls, oak and pine beams and log fires add to the olde worlde atmosphere. Six cottage-style bedrooms provide comfortable accommodation, all with showers, telephone, TV and tea-making facilities. Delicious traditional food is available from the Carvery at lunchtimes and evenings, and the restaurant offers candlelit and à la carte menus, accompanied by a fine wine list. Weekend dinner dances. Les Routiers, Egon Ronay.

£ *Terms on application.*

Suffolk

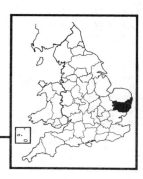

THE SEAFARER HOTEL
Clare, Near Sudbury
0787 277449

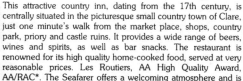

This attractive country inn, dating from the 17th century, is centrally situated in the picturesque small country town of Clare, just one minute's walk from the market place, shops, country park, priory and castle ruins. It provides a wide range of beers, wines and spirits, as well as bar snacks. The restaurant is renowned for its high quality home-cooked food, served at very reasonable prices. Les Routiers, AA High Quality Award, AA/RAC*. The Seafarer offers a welcoming atmosphere and is ideal for holiday touring or short business stopovers.

£ *2 nights (inc. Sat.) full en suite twin/double £24 per person per night bed and breakfast.* ☒ *All year except July and August.*

Staffordshire/Suffolk 91

CLIFF HOUSE
Minsmere Road, Dunwich
072-873 282

A character residence set in 35 acres of mature woodland and providing eight self catering flats. There are also two cottages, a bungalow and a chalet. All cater for two-seven persons and all are fully equipped except for towels and linen. There is a club for residents, furnished with open fires and antique furniture, and another lounge bar. Pool table and darts. Basement games room for children; laundry facilities; shop. Adjacent to Minsmere Bird Sanctuary, this is a conservation area and offers superb opportunities for those who enjoy the outdoor life. Direct access to beach.

[£] *£25 plus VAT per night for minimum of two persons inclusive of heating and lighting.* ⌕ *1 November to 31 March.*

HILL FARM
Kirtling, Newmarket
0638 730253

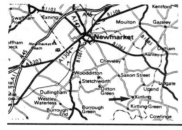

If you want a truly relaxing break in peaceful, rural surroundings, then Hill Farm is the ideal spot. Situated just outside Newmarket, the home of British racing, the farm enjoys extensive rural views of neighbouring stud farms. Guests are assured of good food in comfortable surroundings, with cheerful log fires in cooler weather. Licensed. There are many places of interest within easy travelling distance, including historic Bury St. Edmunds and the beautiful city of Cambridge.

[£] *From £40 double, £55 with dinner.*

GROVE GUEST HOUSE
Grove Road, Woodbridge IP12 4LG
03943 2202

Leslie and Jean Kelly extend a warm welcome to guests wanting to enjoy a few days "away from it all". Grove House is conveniently situated on the A12 at Woodbridge, just a few minutes' drive away from the beautiful Heritage Coast. There is golf and fishing close by, and the area is superb for walking and bird watching. All bedrooms are comfortably furnished, with colour TV and welcome trays. Some have en suite facilities. We offer a choice of menu, and hold a residential licence.

[£] *£42 (inc. VAT) per person for two nights dinner, bed and breakfast. Extra nights pro rata.* ⌕ *All year except Christmas, New Year, and Easter.*

EXPLANATION OF SYMBOLS

TA	Travel Agency Commission
♛	Number of Crowns
⚷	Number of Keys
🐕	Pets Welcome
🐎	Reductions for Children
♿	Suitable for Disabled
🎄	Christmas Breaks

East Sussex

LA VIEILLE AUBERGE RESTAURANT & HOTEL
27 High Street, Battle TN33 0EA
04246 5171

Enjoy a gourmet break at prices no higher than you would pay elsewhere for plain ordinary fare at this fifteenth century inn, rebuilt in 1688 using stone from the old Abbey kitchens. Cosset yourself in our beautiful inglenook restaurant (before a log fire in winter), enjoy a 5-course gastronomic dinner, with wide choices, accompanied by an inexpensive fine wine list. Then relax in an attractively furnished bedroom — one has a four poster bed. All rooms en suite.

£ *From £70 per person for two nights dinner, bed and breakfast. Extra nights pro rata. Prices based on two people sharing a room.* All year.

The Country House at Winchelsea
'Your comfort is our pleasure'

Hastings Road, Winchelsea,
East Sussex, TN36 4AD.
Tel: Rye (0797) 226669

Mary Carmichael

A delightful setting and wonderful country views make our 17th Century listed country house an ideal choice for that 'Special Break'.

Comfortable pretty bedrooms with en-suite or private facilities, colour TV and complimentary hot drinks trays. A cosy sitting room with log fire for those chillier evenings, and in our licensed dining room only the finest local produce is served. Ample parking.

Tariff: Bed and Full English Breakfast £16.50-£18pp.
Pre-booked three course Table d'hôte dinner £10.00pp.
Brochure available.

ETB
Commended

AA "Selected"
Country House   QQQ

AMBLECLIFF HOTEL
35 Upper Rock Gardens, Brighton BN2 1QF
0273 681161

An elegant Victorian hotel (as recommended on TV and in the *Sunday Times*), recently refurbished to very high standards. Highly recommended for cleanliness, comfort and hospitality. AA/RAC Acclaimed. Close to sea, shops, all entertainments and Conference Centre. Attractively decorated rooms with colour TV, central heating, hospitality tray, telephone, hairdryer; majority with en suite toilet. Four-poster beds and non-smoking rooms. Choice of English Breakfast in dining room or Continental breakfast in bed. Access at all times. Supplements for en suites and one night stays.
£ *Bed and breakfast from £16 to £24. Weekly rate 7 nights for the price of 6. Special low season rates.* ☐ *January-December.*

COLSON HOUSE HOTEL
17 Upper Rock Gardens, Brighton BN2 1QE
0273 694922

Colson House is a small charming hotel dating back to the fashionable days of the Prince Regent, and retains many of the original features throughout. Centrally located for the Conference Centre, Lanes, Royal Pavilion and all Brighton's entertainments. All bedrooms have private bath/shower en suite, colour TV, and tea/coffee facilities. Twin, family, double or single rooms available. Centrally heated throughout. With its unique character and reputation, Colson House welcomes guests from all over the world, and whether your stay is for business or pleasure, we are sure it will be enjoyable.
£ *Two or three days breaks: Bed and breakfast from £15 per person per night, evening meal £7.50.* ☐ *All year.*

KEMPTON HOUSE HOTEL
33/34 Marine Parade, Brighton BN2 1TR
0273 570248

AA and RAC Highly Acclaimed. We are a private seafront hotel offering a relaxed and friendly holiday or a short break. Rooms available with magnificent views overlooking beach and pier. Rooms with full en suite shower and toilet with central heating, direct-dial telephone, colour TV, radio/clock alarm, hairdryer and tea/coffee facilities. Full English breakfast served or Continental in bed. Four-poster room available overlooking sea. Residents' bar and sea-facing patio garden for your use. Ideally suited for business or pleasure. Please telephone for details.
£ *From £20 per person per night for bed and breakfast. Dinner available by prior arrangement.* ☐ *Open all year.*

ST CATHERINES LODGE HOTEL
Kingsway, Hove, Brighton BN3 2RZ
0273 778181 Telex 877073

A well established sea-front hotel with fine Regency features. It was formerly the home of a wealthy Dutch merchant. Its excellent restaurant specialises in fine European cuisine and there is an attractive cocktail bar and a garden. The guest rooms — two with four poster beds — all have television and direct-dial facilities, most have private facilities. There is a games room, while opposite the hotel is the new King Alfred Leisure Centre with water slides and pools. Extensive shopping and entertainment nearby. AA**, RAC***.
£ *£68-£72 for any two nights dinner, bed and breakfast in room without bath; £80-£90 for room with bath.* ☐ *All year.*

THE WHITE HOUSE
6 Bedford Street, Brighton BN2 1AN
0273 607576

This delightful, family-run Regency Hotel enjoys an excellent position near the promenade, marina and town centre. Close to Conference Centre — ideal for those attending conferences or exhibitions. All rooms en suite, with central heating, colour TV and tea/coffee facilities. Full English breakfast or vegetarian breakfast as required. Special low season offers — tariff and brochure on request. ETB registered, Member Brighton Guest House Association.

£ *Bed and breakfast from £17.50 to £24. Reductions for weekly stays.*

PEKES
Chiddingly, Hailsham BN27 4AD
071-352 8088

Commended
♛♛♛♛ / ♛♛♛♛♛

In the grounds of a 16th century Tudor manor house with unspoilt views of the Sussex countryside, Pekes offers a unique self-catering holiday. Peaceful, yet close to London, with exceptional facilities — indoor heated swimming pool, sauna/jacuzzi, sunbed/exercise room and hard tennis court. A large oast house sleeps seven to eleven; three period cottages sleep four to six. All very well equipped with colour TV, full central heating, washing machines, tumble dryers, fridge/freezers amd dishwashers. Children welcome, pets by arrangement.

£ *3 night weekend breaks and 4 night midweek breaks from £124 to £276.* ◫ *October 29, 1990 to March 22, 1991 (except Christmas and New Year). Enquire about "Last Minute" Summer Breaks 1991.*

BEAUPORT PARK HOTEL
Battle Road, Hastings TN38 8EA
0424 851222

♛♛♛♛ TA

This fine three-star country house hotel, standing in 33 acres of its own grounds, offers old-fashioned personal service from resident directors Kenneth and Helena Melsom. AA, RAC. All bedrooms are very well equipped, and all are en suite. The hotel has a heated outdoor pool, tennis courts, croquet, a putting green, and country walks, while squash, golf, and riding can all be enjoyed nearby. Country House Bargain Breaks available all year.

£ *£72-£84 per person for two nights, Friday to Sunday dinner, bed and breakfast. £240-£274 for four nights, Monday to Thursday dinner, bed and breakfast.* ◫ *All year.*

THE ROSE AND CROWN INN
Fletching Street, Mayfield TN20 6TE
0435 872200

Set in the historic village of Mayfield, this lovely old inn has been used by wayfarers and travellers for the last 500 years. Bedrooms are well appointed, with colour TV and tea/coffee making facilities. Bar meals can be enjoyed in the garden or in any of the four bars, and restaurant meals are available throughout the day and evening. The Rose and Crown won an Egon Ronay Award in 1983, and is recommended in many pub guides. The coast, Ashdown Forest, Tunbridge Wells etc are all within easy reach.

£ *Terms on application.*

East Sussex 95

RIVERDALE PRIVATE HOTEL
Alfriston, Polegate BN26 5TR
0323 870397

A small hotel in the country set in a peaceful and elevated position on the South Downs with clear and breathtaking views. RAC Acclaimed. The culinary emphasis is on English cooking by the resident proprietor, and the hotel caters for vegetarians if notice is given at booking time. Riverdale grows its own vegetables and soft fruits, and has its own supply of fresh eggs. Table licence. Most of the individual and well furnished bedrooms are en suite and each has colour TV, clock, radio, trouser press, hairdryer, and radiator.

£ *From £66-£74 for two nights dinner, bed and breakfast. Shorter or longer breaks on request.*

BROOMHILL LODGE
Rye Foreign, Near Rye TN31 7UN
07978 421

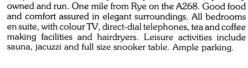

Early nineteenth century country house hotel, privately owned and run. One mile from Rye on the A268. Good food and comfort assured in elegant surroundings. All bedrooms en suite, with colour TV, direct-dial telephones, tea and coffee making facilities and hairdryers. Leisure activities include sauna, jacuzzi and full size snooker table. Ample parking.

£ *Enjoy a midweek break any 2 consecutive nights Monday to Friday a.m. Extra nights pro rata. Weekend breaks also available.*

JEAKE'S HOUSE
Mermaid Street, Rye TN31 7ET
0797 222828

This beautiful listed building, once the 'deeply cherished' home of author Conrad Aiken, was built by Samuel Jeake in 1689. It stands in one of England's most famous streets, renowned for its cobblestoned charm and association with notorious smugglers. Traditional and vegetarian breakfast is served in the 18th century galleried former chapel. Oak-beamed and panelled bedrooms overlooking the marsh and roof tops to the sea, are furnished with brass or mahogany beds, linen sheets and lace, and have en suite facilities, TV, radio, telephone and hot drinks trays. Four-poster suite available. AA Selected, RAC listed. Access, Visa, Mastercard accepted.

£ *£18-£24 per day for two nights bed and breakfast. Reductions for four or more nights. All year.*

WHITEHOUSE FARM HOLIDAY HOMES
Nutley, Uckfield TN22 3EE
082571 2377

Commended

These delightful, fully equipped holiday homes are situated on a small working farm overlooking the beautiful Ashdown Forest, home of the fictional bear, Winnie the Pooh. All units have two bedrooms; free duvets and bed linen included. Large lounge/diner with colour TV; spacious kitchen with washer/dryer, fridge/freezer etc. All furniture and fittings are solid pine. The accommodation is fully double glazed and insulated; free heating by electric storage/convectors. Within easy reach of London and the coast. Local activities include riding, fishing and walking. ETB Approved. Brochure on request.

£ *3 day breaks: midweek £96; including weekends £120. October to March inclusive.*

96 *East Sussex*

THE COUNTRY HOUSE at WINCHELSEA
Hastings Road, Winchelsea TN36 4AD
0797 226669

Commended

AA "Selected" **QQQ** Country House. Lovely countryside, much of it National Trust, surrounds our 17th century former Sussex Farmhouse. Situated in its own grounds, many species of butterflies and birds find a haven in the old walled garden. A house full of character and charm, with spacious rooms and delightful views, but with all the comforts that one expects of today. The individually styled bedrooms offer en-suite or private facilities, remote control colour television and complimentary hot drinks trays. A warmly inviting lounge and elegant dining room; all go to make this 'Country House' a delightful break.

£ *For 2 nights or more dinner, bed and breakfast in a luxury en suite room for 2 persons sharing, £112.*

West Sussex

BLACK MILL HOUSE HOTEL

Princess Avenue
West BOGNOR REGIS
Telephone 0243 821945

AA   RAC
Ashley Courtenay Recommended
SE England Tourist Board

The hotel is family run, situated in the quieter west end of the town, 300 yards from the Sea and Marine Gardens. There are 26 bedrooms, 18 with bathrooms/shower, all with radio, colour television, telephone and tea and coffee making facilities. Restaurant, cocktail bar, lounges, games room with small snooker table, table tennis and darts. Large enclosed garden, own car park. Children special offers – under two years free; dogs welcome. Ample car parking. An excellent centre for touring the South, and visiting the Mary Rose, The Warrior, Victory, Wildfowl Trust, Goodwood House, Open Air Museum, Fishbourne Roman Palace and Arundel Castle. From £52 to £60 for any two nights, dinner, bed and breakfast. Applicable October 1 to March 28. Also Spring, April 2 to May 24 1991 and Summer Short Breaks available. Open all year and Christmas. TA

BURPHAM COUNTRY HOTEL
Burpham, Arundel
0903 882160

A charming country house hotel, dating from c.1710, and enjoying superb downland views. AA*, Ashley Courtenay. En suite bedrooms are spacious and well furnished, and all have colour television and tea and coffee making facilities. The hotel's licensed restaurant serves fresh local produce, and vegetarian dishes are available. This is an ideal base from which to see the beauties of the South Downs — Burpham itself is a picturesque Sussex village, and the Arun Valley is ideal for walkers.

[£] *From £34.50 per day per person.* ⌧ *October to May excluding Christmas, Easter and Bank Holidays.*

MILL HOUSE HOTEL
Ashington RH20 3BZ
0903 892426

A delightful small country house hotel well placed to take advantage of the places of interest and sporting amenities which West Sussex has to offer. AA**. A relaxed atmosphere prevails throughout, while service is skilful yet friendly. Guest rooms are equipped with modern amenities including colour television and direct dial telephone. Log fires burn in the lounges in winter, and there is an attractive cocktail bar in which to spend a relaxing evening.

[£] *£85 per person for two-night weekend break of dinner, bed and breakfast; 3-day break including Sunday £115 per person.* ⌧ *All year, not Bank Holidays.*

BLACK MILL HOUSE HOTEL
Bognor Regis, West Sussex PO21 2QU
0243 821945

The hotel is family run, situated in the quieter west end of the town, 300 yards from the sea and Marine Gardens. Ashley Courtenay Recommended. Attractive enclosed gardens. There are 26 bedrooms, 18 with private bathroom. All have radio, colour television, telephone and tea/coffee making facilities. Restaurant, cocktail bar, lounges, games room with small snooker table, table tennis and darts. Ample car parking. An excellent centre for touring the south and visiting the Mary Rose, The Warrior, Victory and Arundel Castle. Member S.E. England Tourist Board.

[£] *From £52-£60 for any 2 nights dinner, bed and breakfast, applicable October 1 to March 28. Spring Breaks (April 2–May 24) £58-£66 and Summer Short Breaks available. Open all year including Christmas.*

CHEQUERS HOTEL
Church Place, Pulborough RH20 1AD
079-82 2486

Chequers is a Queen Anne country house tastefully modernised, yet retaining old world charm and comforts. AA, RAC**. Cosy log fires in winter complement the warmth of the welcome guests receive. En suite bedrooms, all with colour TV, direct-dial telephone, trouser press, hairdryer and tea/coffee facilities. Four-poster rooms and ground floor rooms available. The restaurant serves fresh market produce from a daily-changing menu. New garden conservatory, car park. Superb position overlooking the South Downs.

[£] *£65 per person for TWO nights dinner, bed and breakfast until 31 March 1991; thereafter £70. Extra nights at further reduced rates. Special weekly terms on request.*

Tyne & Wear

DENE HOTEL
40-42 Grosvenor Road, Newcastle-upon-Tyne NE2 2RP
091-281 1502/8110

The fully licensed hotel is pleasantly situated in the quiet residential area of Jesmond, yet is only four minutes from the city centre, university, polytechnic and the huge Eldon Square shopping precinct. Most rooms have showers; all have washbasins, colour televisions and tea/coffee making facilities. The hotel is fully centrally heated. Car park.

£ *Single from £17.50, double from £35 per night; dinner from £4.50.* All year.

THE BEAMISH PARK HOTEL
Beamish Burn Road, Marley Hill, Newcastle-upon-Tyne NE16 5EU
0207 230666/7

In the heart of the countryside, approximately one mile from the Beamish Museum and 4 miles from the Gateshead Metro Centre. All bedrooms are en suite, with tea/coffee making facilities, colour TV, radio, hairdryer, trouser press and direct-dial telephone. AA/RAC***. The hotel offers a choice of either the À La Carte restaurant or the Conservatory Bistro. Literally on the doorstep you will find the Causey Arch Pub, a traditional British pub and a well-known landmark. Write or phone for our colour brochure and details of our Bargain Break weekends.

£ *Minimum of 2 consecutive weekend nights: £19.50 per night bed and breakfast, £27.50 per night dinner, bed and breakfast.*

THE GIBSIDE ARMS HOTEL
Front Street, Whickham NE16 4JJ
091-488 9292 Fax: 0207 281260

Set in the old village centre of Whickham, this modern, 45-bedroomed hotel offers an ideal touring base. AA/RAC***. The hotel has magnificent views over the Tyne Valley, including the Gateshead Metro Centre which is less than 1½ miles away. All bedrooms are en suite, with tea/coffee making facilities, trouser press, hairdryer, satellite TV and radio. The Strathmore Restaurant offers a fine table d'hôte menu as well as an excellent à la carte menu. Ring or write now for our colour brochure and details of our Bargain Break Weekends.

£ *Minimum of 2 consecutive weekend nights: bed and breakfast £19.50 per person per night; dinner, bed and breakfast £27.50 per person per night.*

Warwickshire

FOLLY FARM COTTAGE
Ilmington, Shipston on Stour CV36 4LJ
060-882 425

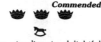
Commended

Luxury old world country cottage standing in delightful gardens overlooking village orchard. Situated in the truly unspoilt Cotswold village of Ilmington, nestling at the foot of the Campden Hills and ideal for visiting Stratford-upon-Avon or surrounding Cotswold villages. Luxurious accommodation is in twin or four-poster rooms, with antique furniture, radio, colour TV, tea making facilities, and en suite bathrooms with corner shower tubs. Superb breakfast is served in the privacy of your room. Excellent pub or restaurant food available within walking distance. Fantastic quality at realistic prices.
£ *Bed and breakfast from £15.00 per person per night.*
Open all year.

Sequoia House
PRIVATE HOTEL

Sequoia House is superbly situated across the River Avon opposite the Royal Shakespeare Theatre. It has recently been modernised to a high standard and offers guests excellent facilities with charmingly appointed accommodation, good food, and the friendly and personal attention of the resident proprietors. Each bedroom has colour TV, tea and coffee making facilities, and telephone. Most have private facilities, with toilet and bath or shower. There is a delightful garden walk to the Theatre, riverside gardens, Shakespeare properties, shops, and leisure complex. Sequoia House is licensed. Large private car park for guests' use. *Theatre booking service available.*

51 SHIPSTON ROAD
STRATFORD UPON AVON CV37 7LN
TEL: (0789) 68852

Bed & Breakfast
from £16.50 to £29.50

Moonraker House

More than **50%** of our guests are on their 2nd, 3rd, 4th . . . visit. Come and see why!

* ALL rooms are elegantly decorated and designed with your comfort in mind
* CAR PARK (open and garage)
* Ideal centre for exploring the Cotswolds, Shakespeare's Countryside, Warwick Castle and Shakespeare Theatres
* ALL rooms have ensuite bathrooms, tea and coffee making facilities, colour TV, clock radios and fitted hairdryers
* There are also extra special rooms with FOUR POSTER BEDS, lounge area and garden patio (non-smoking)
* Enjoy an excellent English Breakfast prepared with care by the resident proprietors

Mauveen and Mike Spencer.

40 Alcester Road
Stratford-upon-Avon CV37 9DB
Tel: (0789) 299346
Fax: (0789) 295504

AA
QQQ

MinOtels
Les Routiers

HALFORD BRIDGE INN
Fosse Way, Halford, Shipston-on-Stour CV36 5BN
0789 740382

This charming sixteenth century inn is only 8 miles from Stratford-upon-Avon, and so is ideally placed for touring Shakespeare country, visiting theatres etc. AA, Egon Ronay and Les Routiers Recommended. The restaurant has recently been renovated, and this lovely room forms a very fitting background for the excellent fare offered at most reasonable prices. Each of the five bedrooms has a washbasin and colour TV, and three have showers. Local activities include fishing, walking, and horse-racing at Warwick and Stratford. Tony and Greta Westwood offer guests excellent value for money and good food in a relaxing atmosphere.

£ ☼ *On application.*

SEQUOIA HOUSE PRIVATE HOTEL
51 Shipston Road, Stratford-upon-Avon
0789 68852

Sequoia House is superbly situated across the River Avon opposite the Royal Shakespeare Theatre. Each bedroom has colour television, tea and coffee making facilities, and a telephone. Most have private facilities. Sequoia is licensed and is known for its friendly and personal attention given by the resident proprietors. Large private car park.

£ *Bed and breakfast from £16.50 to £29.50.* ☼ *All year.*

HUNTERS MOON GUEST HOUSE
150 Alcester Road, Stratford-on-Avon CV37 9DR
0789 292888 (reservations) 0789 204101 (guests)

Hunters Moon has been operated by the same family for over 30 years, and has recently been completely modernised and refurbished. We can now offer hotel-type accommodation at guest house prices. Single, double, twin and family rooms are offered, with private facilities, fitted hair dryers, dual voltage shaver points, tea and coffee making facilities and colour TV. Orthopaedic beds also available on request. TV lounge. Free parking. Single night bookings available. Arthur Frommer Recommended. AA Listed. Visa, Access, American Express and JCB cards accepted.

£ *Room with shower £11.50; with shower and toilet £12.50.* ☼ *October 31st to March 31st, except Christmas. Minimum 2 nights.*

CHURCH FARM
Dorsington, Stratford-upon-Avon
0789 720471 and 0831 504194

A warm welcome awaits all guests at Church Farm, an attractive Georgian farmhouse with central heating for all year round comfort. Guests are free to explore this mixed working farm. Gliding, fishing, boating, and horse riding are all available nearby. Bedrooms are comfortable (some en suite in converted stable block) with tea/coffee making facilities and TV. Church Farm is within easy driving distance of Stratford, Warwick Castle, and the Cotswolds. AA.

£ *From £11.50 per person per night for bed and breakfast.* ☼ *All year.*

MOONRAKER HOUSE
40 Alcester Road, Stratford-on-Avon CV37 9DB
0789 67115/299346

Situated on the north side of the town, Moonraker House has family, double and twin rooms all en suite with co-ordinated decor and furnishings, central heating, colour TV, hairdryers, radios and beverage making facilities. De-luxe rooms with four-poster beds and luxury suite available. Good food prepared by resident proprietors. Hotel facilities at guest house prices. Ideally situated for exploring Shakespeare country and the Cotswolds. AA recommended.

[£] *Prices on application.* [☐] *All year.*

West Midlands

BARON'S COURT HOTEL & RESTAURANT
Walsall Wood, Near Lichfield WS9 9AH
0543 452020

Baron's Court, an Olde Worlde Tudor style hotel, is situated on the A461 midway between Walsall and historic Lichfield, which is four miles away. The hotel boasts an indoor Health Hydro with swimming pool, steam and sauna rooms, fitness centre etc. AA***, RAC***. There are 100 Queen Anne style bedrooms, all with private facilities and there are also many four poster suites, so it is little wonder that one of the hotel's specialities is romantic weekend breaks. Each Saturday there is a dinner dance, always with a superb atmosphere.

[£] *Two nights dinner, bed and breakfast from £75 per person.*

PUBLISHER'S NOTE

While every effort is made to ensure accuracy, we regret that FHG Publications cannot accept responsibility for errors, omissions or misrepresentation in our entries or any consequences thereof. Prices in particular should be checked because we go to press early. We will follow up complaints but cannot act as arbiters or agents for either party.

Wiltshire

NETTLETON ARMS
Nettleton, Chippenham SN14 7NP
0249 782783

Once the manor house of the Codrington family, this early 16th century establishment still has the air of a cherished private residence, with its fine furnishings, polished wood, minstrels' gallery and well-tended log fire. Guests are accommodated in the converted medieval barn, and all bedrooms are exceedingly well appointed, with en suite facilities. Quality bar lunches and suppers are served, with an extensive menu to suit all tastes. Egon Ronay.

£ *Weekends (Friday or Saturday) 2 nights, including 3-course meal and bottle of wine £85; mid-week 2 nights bed and breakfast £67.50.*

THE WHITE HART INN
Ford, Chippenham SN14 8RP
0249 782213

Idyllically situated by a trout stream and overlooking the lush Weavern Valley is the 16th century White Hart Inn. AA**, RAC**. An old stone built pub with beams and log fires, it offers a relaxing and peaceful short break. All rooms are furnished in keeping with the inn's character, and all are en suite. Many delicious and old-fashioned recipes have been found to delight guests in the Riverside Restaurant, and good wines and real ale are offered. Outdoor swimming pool and shrubbery. Near Castle Combe, reputedly the most beautiful of England's villages.

£ *£162 for a two person two day break; £243 for three days.* ☐ *All year.*

THE RUDLOE PARK HOTEL
Leafy Lane, Corsham SN13 0PA
0225 810555

This 1850 Neo-Gothic Victorian mansion is set in four acres of award-winning gardens offering views down Box Valley to the Georgian city of Bath. The highly recommended Cameo Restaurant serves an excellent variety of good fresh food, with the tasteful decor, comfortable chairs and chandeliers creating a relaxed atmosphere of good living. All bedrooms are individually designed and decorated, and have private bathrooms, direct-dial telephones, colour television and tea/coffee facilities. Ideally situated for visiting Bath, the Cotswolds and the West Country. AA and RAC***. Egon Ronay, Michelin, Ashley Courtenay, BTA Commended.

£ *Dinner, bed and breakfast, 2 nights £100 per person sharing double room.* ☐ *Not Christmas or Bank Holidays.*

BEAR HOTEL
Devizes SN10 1HS
0380 722444

Famous old coaching inn overlooking the attractive market square. AA***, Egon Ronay, Ashley Courtenay, Michelin, Relais Routiers. All 25 rooms are en suite, with colour TV, radio, direct-dial telephones, beverage making facilities and hairdryers. Visiting hairdresser/beautician by arrangement. Two restaurants, two bars, lounge and TV room. Devizes is an old market town, with many fascinating buildings and old inns. Bath, Salisbury, Longleat and Stonehenge are all within easy reach.

£ *£80 per person for 2 nights bed, breakfast and £14.00 allowance towards dinner. Single supplement.* ❑ *Not Bank Holidays, Christmas or New Year.*

THE BECKFORD ARMS
Fonthill Gifford, Tisbury, Salisbury SP3 6PX
0747 870385

The charming 18th century Beckford Arms lies in fine rolling countryside in an area of outstanding natural beauty. Easily reached are the cathedral city of Salisbury, the seaside town of Bournemouth, Bath, Stonehenge, Longleat, Stourhead Gardens and other places of interest. The Beckford Arms boasts seven tastefully furnished bedrooms, all with modern facilities including en suite bathrooms, colour television etc. Some have four-poster beds. Friendly bars and restaurant provide log fires, real ales, good food and fine wines. 2 miles from Tisbury station and A303. CAMRA "Beer, Bed and Breakfast".

£ *2 nights dinner, bed and breakfast including one bottle of sparkling wine from £49.50 per person.* ❑ *Any day excluding Christmas and Easter.*

Worcestershire

CHEQUERS INN
Fladbury, Pershore WR10 2PZ
0386 860276

The Chequers, standing at the end of a quiet lane in the peaceful village of Fladbury, offers exceptional accommodation, good food and hospitality. It is warm and comfortable, with a traditional country lounge bar with magnificent open fire, a cosy restaurant and eight delightful bedrooms. The inn enjoys a fine reputation for its food, and fresh local fruit and vegetables are used wherever possible in bar meals, traditional Sunday lunches and in the restaurant and carvery. Ideal for the lovely Vale of Evesham. Superb angling free to guests.

£ *Any 2 nights bed and breakfast £48 per person, any 3 nights £70.* ❑ *Not Christmas or Bank Holiday weekends.*

MOUNT PLEASANT HOTEL
Belle Vue Terrace, Great Malvern WR14 4PZ
0684 561837

This elegant Georgian building (circa 1730) has been entirely refurbished, with all modern comforts, all rooms being en suite, with television, direct-dial telephone and tea/coffee making facilities. Great Malvern, which lies seven miles south west of Worcester, is beautifully situated on the slopes of the Malvern Hills. The hotel is centrally located, overlooking the majestic priory church. Fully licensed, with excellent bar and restaurant meals. There is direct access to the hills through the one and a half acres of gardens. Les Routiers and Michelin recommended.
£ **£65 per person for 2 nights bed, breakfast and dinner (1st November 1990 to 31st March 1991); £74 from 1st April 1991. Extra nights pro rata.**

ROCK HOUSE
144 West Malvern Road, Malvern WR14 4NJ
0684 574536

Commended

Family-run, early Victorian Guest House, situated high on hills in peaceful atmosphere with superb views over 40 miles. Les Routiers Recommended. Ideal rambling centre for hills or open country. Eleven comfortable bedrooms, all with wash-basins, most overlooking our splendid view. TV room and quiet room. Licensed to enhance the excellent cuisine. Groups and active elderly welcome. Parking on premises. Please send stamp for brochure.
£ **Special autumn/winter breaks: any three days mid-week dinner, bed and breakfast £57 per person inc. VAT.**

LENCHFORD HOTEL
Shrawley, Worcester WR6 6TB
0905 620229

Situated on the banks of the River Severn in the picturesque village of Shrawley midway between Worcester and Stourport on the B4196. AA***, RAC***. The 16 bedrooms are well appointed, all with colour TV, and almost all are en suite. The hotel has two restaurants and two bars. Moorings are available for boats at the hotel's own landing stage, and there is a swimming pool for guests' use. Barbecues are held on Friday evenings throughout the summer. The hotel's situation near the Shropshire and Hereford and Worcester borders, makes it an ideal base for sightseeing.
£ **£36 per person per night for dinner, bed and breakfast; minimum stay two nights.** All year.

EXPLANATION OF SYMBOLS

TA	Travel Agency Commission
♛	Number of Crowns
⚲	Number of Keys
🐕	Pets Welcome
🐎	Reductions for Children
♿	Suitable for Disabled
🎄	Christmas Breaks

106 *Worcestershire*

North Yorkshire

KING'S ARMS HOTEL AND RESTAURANT
Market Place, Askrigg in Wensleydale DL8 3HQ
0969 50258 Fax: 0969 50635

This ancient, listed coaching inn, featured in BBC's "All Creatures Great and Small", faces the famous TV vet's house across the market square of Askrigg. All bedrooms are en suite, and have colour TV, radio, phone, tea/coffee making facilities and feature antique poster/canopy beds. The à la carte restaurant serves the finest English cuisine and offers an award-winning wine list. Bar meals are served lunchtimes and evenings, along with a selection of real ales. Come and savour the peace and beauty of the Dales; linger awhile and discover the special magic of the North. AA**, RAC**, Ashley Courtenay, Egon Ronay, Les Routiers, Johanssen, Good Pub, Hotel and Beer Guides.

£ *Terms on application.*

ROSE AND CROWN HOTEL
Bainbridge, Wensleydale DL8 3EE
0969 50225

This 15th century hotel is situated in the lovely Wensleydale village of Bainbridge, which has a village green complete with a set of stocks. It offers a warm and friendly atmosphere, with log fires, beamed ceilings, and antique furnishings. There are 12 pretty en suite bedrooms, and in the restaurant the emphasis is on traditional food with the best local produce. This is an ideal centre for touring, walking, fishing or simply enjoying the beautiful countryside of the Dales National Park. AA**, RAC**. Egon Ronay, Johansen, Signpost, Good Food Guide.

£ *Dinner, bed and breakfast for two or three day breaks from £36 per person per night.*

THE OLD RECTORY
Thormanby, Easingwold, York YO6 3WN
0845 401417

A warm welcome awaits you at this 18th century Georgian rectory which is furnished with many antiques, including a four-poster bed. There are 3 comfortable and spacious bedrooms with washbasins, a charming lounge with colour TV and open fire, and a separate dining room. This is an excellent base for touring the Moors, Dales, York and "Herriot" country, with many historic houses and abbeys in the area. York 17 miles. Many delightful inns and restaurants serving good food locally. Ample private parking. Open all year.

£ *From £23 per person for 2 nights bed and breakfast.*
Off-season.

WHITFIELD HOUSE HOTEL
Goathland, Whitby
0947 86215

On the fringe of Goathland in the beautiful North York Moors, this residentially licensed, family run hotel has 10 bedrooms, all with en suite bathrooms. All bedrooms have tea/coffee making facilities and radio. Central heating throughout. It offers a friendly atmosphere, with colour television lounge and excellent food. Ideally situated for walking or touring the National Park, the North York Moors Railway is close by, and Whitby and the coast is just nine miles away. AA*, Les Routiers, Guestaccom.

£ *Dinner, bed and breakfast from £25 per person per day, minimum 2 nights.* ☐ *January to April (excluding Easter); October and November.*

NEW LAITHE HOUSE
Wood Lane, Grassington, Skipton BD23 5LU
0756 752764

A converted barn, situated in the heart of Wharfedale offering the ideal of the countryside and solitude of a quiet village in Yorkshire. Rooms are centrally heated with colour television and tea making facilities. Most rooms are en suite. Grassington is the ideal base for visiting the many historic towns in Yorkshire. There is a private car park where you can leave your car and go walking or fishing for the day and enjoy the splendid scenery on foot.

£ *From £30-£36 per person, bed and breakfast, for any two nights.* ☐ *31 October to 31 May excluding Christmas, New Year, Easter and Bank Holidays.*

THE GRANBY HOTEL
Granby Road, Harrogate HG1 4SR
0423 506151

Situated overlooking Harrogate's famous Stray Parkland, the three-star rated Granby Hotel is an ideal base for visiting many of Yorkshire's splendid attractions. The Dales, Skipton and York are all within a short drive and Harrogate itself has many interesting places. All 93 bedrooms have private facilities. There is a cocktail bar and a choice of two restaurants. Excellent car parking.

£ *Dinner, bed and breakfast £45 per person per night; bed and breakfast £35 per person per night. "Sneak a Week" – stay for 7 nights, pay for 6 – dinner, bed and breakfast £270 per person.* ☐ *Available April 1 1991 to March 31 1992.*

THE LANGHAM HOTEL
Valley Drive, Harrogate HG2 0JL
0423 502179

Beautiful old hotel, owned and managed by the Ward families. Also exquisite restaurant offering superb cuisine. All bedrooms have private bathroom, radio, colour TV, telephone and tea/coffee making facilities. Contact Stephen Ward for brochure and details of Spa Breaks. Les Routiers.

£ *£36.00 per person per night sharing a twin/double room for bed, full English breakfast and dinner. Single supplement £5.50.* ☐ *All year, subject to availability.*

YOUNG'S HOTEL
15 York Road, Harrogate HG1 2QL
0423 567336/521231

A comfortable family run hotel offering a high standard of accommodation and service. All 16 bedrooms have en suite bath or shower room, colour television, direct dial telephone and tea and coffee making facilities. The hotel stands in half-an-acre of attractive gardens in the quiet Duchy area and within easy walking distance of the town centre. Ample parking is available. An ideal base for touring the Yorkshire Dales and many surrounding places of interest. Please telephone for further information.

£ *From £30.50 per night for dinner, bed and breakfast. Weekly from £195.* ◻ *All year except Conference/Exhibition periods.*

SIMONSTONE HALL
Hawes, North Yorkshire DL8 3LY
0969 667255 Fax: 0969 667741

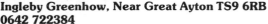

Elegant, 250-year-old country house hotel enjoying unsurpassed views across James Herriot's Wensleydale. Comfortably furnished with antiques giving the aura and grace of a bygone age, but with all the essential luxuries of the twentieth century. Excellent cuisine, extensive wine list. All rooms en suite with colour TV and teamakers. Christmas and New Year house parties. Dogs welcome. Personally managed by the resident owners Mr and Mrs A. Jeffryes and their family. Winner of RAC Blue Ribbon Award 1988 and 1989. Self-catering studio for two people also available.

£ *2 nights dinner, bed and breakfast from £84 per night for 2 people.*

MANOR HOUSE FARM
Ingleby Greenhow, Near Great Ayton TS9 6RB
0642 722384

A charming old farmhouse in a picturesque setting amidst delightful parkland, hills, and woodland. Accommodation is of the highest standard, with all modern comforts. Fine dinners are served by candlelight and complemented by excellent wines, and the log fires add to the tranquil and welcoming atmosphere. Manor House Farm stands in the North York Moors National Park, with the delights of York, Herriot Country, and Castle Howard all nearby. Children and pets by arrangement.

£ *From £27.50 per person per day for two or more nights dinner, bed and breakfast.* ◻ *All year.*

NEWTON HOUSE HOTEL
5/7 York Place, Knaresborough, Near Harrogate HG5 0AD
0423 863539

Commended

Newton House is a privately owned hotel in a beautiful Grade II listed building, only two minutes' walk from the market square of this historic town. RAC Highly Acclaimed. AA. The 12 en suite bedrooms all have colour TV, beverage making facilities, mini-bar and telephone. For that special romantic break there are four-poster rooms. Local attractions include golf, horse-racing, fishing and walking over the beautiful Yorkshire Dales only ½ an hour's drive. Historic York is only 20 minutes away, Harrogate 10 minutes.

£ *£50 per couple, incl. full English breakfast. Dinner for 2 FREE on Saturday night when staying Fri/Sat or Sat/Sun, or 3rd night free when staying any 2 nights Sun-Thurs (not Fri/Sat).* ◻ *November to March 31 except Bank Holidays, trade fairs, exhibitions.*

HARROW INGS COUNTRY HOUSE
Lothersdale, Near Skipton BD20 8HR
0535 636658

"Shangri La is true — it's here" one of our guests remarked. Charming old farmhouse, barn and shepherd's cottages, lovingly restored, boasting exposed stonework, beamed ceilings, mullions, polished floors and antiques. Surrounded by beautiful Dales countryside and breathtaking views, perfect for sightseeing Bronte, Herriot and Pendlewitch country, golfing, walking (Pennine Way ½ mile) or relaxing in our peace and tranquillity. Luxurious accommodation to the highest standard in Laura Ashley. All rooms have tea making facilities and television, and most are en suite. No smoking. You will adore the "Harrow Ings" experience — everyone does!
£ *Bed and breakfast from £15 per person. Weekly terms available.* ☼ *Open all year.*

YORKSHIRE PROPERTIES
Black Carr House, Skipton Road, Colne, Lancashire BB8 8QU
0282 869404

Luxury stone self-catering cottages, superbly equipped. ETB and Yorkshire Tourist Board Approved. Linen and towels provided, no hidden extras. Central heating, colour TV and video, dishwashers, microwaves etc. Properties sleep from 2 to 14 persons. Settle is a historic market town and the Gateway to the Dales. It is a superb base for touring the Lakes, York and the West Coast. Skipton has many sporting facilities including a swimming pool.

£ *Short Breaks available out of season (November to March, not including Christmas and New Year).*

THE WENSLEYDALE HEIFER
West Witton, Leyburn DL8 4LS
0969 22322

A 17th century inn of character and distinction offering, quite simply, Wensleydale's best, together with the finest of Yorkshire innkeeping traditions. Situated amidst spectacular James Herriot countryside in the magnificent Yorkshire Dales National Park. Finest Yorkshire cuisine is served in the candlelit restaurant and bistro, along with a selection of real ales and fine wines. AA/RAC**, Egon Ronay, Michelin, Les Routiers, Johansens. 19 en suite bedrooms, 3 four-poster suites. A wide range of activity breaks on offer include trout fishing, golfing, James Herriot trail, walking and "romantic". Christmas and New Year house party.
£ *Terms on application.*

WELGARTH HOUSE
Wetherby Road, Rufforth, York YO2 3QB
0904-83 592 or 595

AA Listed. Welgarth House is an individual and most attractive detached house, situated in the delightful village of Rufforth, five minutes' drive from the historic city of York. Ideal touring base for the North Yorkshire Moors, the Yorkshire Dales and East Coast resorts. All rooms have vanity units, colour TV and tea/coffee making facilities. En suite available. Residents' lounge and separate dining room. Self-catering holidays available; also shooting, fishing and gliding. Phone or write for brochure.

£ *Bed and breakfast from £13, reductions early and late season.*

CLIFTON GREEN HOTEL
8 Clifton Green, York YO3 6LH
0904 623597

Clifton Green Hotel, privately owned and managed, is situated in a conservation area of Clifton, overlooking Clifton Green and within walking distance of the City centre and York Minster. Spacious bedrooms, some with en-suite facilities and all with colour television. The owner gives careful attention to the comfort and needs of her guests. Private parking.

£ *Bed and breakfast from £15 per person per night.*
All year.

INGLEWOOD GUEST HOUSE
7 Clifton Green, York YO3 6LH
0904 653523

The Inglewood Guest House has a warm and friendly atmosphere where guests will really feel at home. Bedrooms all have colour TV; some en suite bathrooms. Breakfast is an enjoyable experience in the pleasant dining room. It is an ideal centre for exploring York and making day excursions to the many market towns and attractive villages around the city. Helpful information on where to go and what to see provided on request. A car is not essential, but parking is available. Open all year with central heating.

£ *Bed and breakfast from £15.*

KNAVESMIRE MANOR HOTEL
302 Tadcaster Road, York YO2 2HE
0904 702941

This fine Georgian hotel, which dates from around 1833, was once a home of the Rowntree family. It is prettily sited close to York racecourse and convenient for the centre of the city, with its wealth of tourist attractions. A choice of hotel or motel rooms is offered, all en suite, with telephone, radio, TV and welcome tray. Leisure facilities include a tropical swimming pool and a health spa located in the walled gardens. Arnold's Restaurant offers rather special cuisine. Car park. RAC/AA**.

£ *Terms on application.*

LADY ANNE MIDDLETON'S HOTEL
Skeldergate, York YO1 1DS
0904 632257/630456/611570

This historic hotel is set in English gardens close to the river and in the heart of the fascinating City of York. All rooms are en suite, with television, telephone and tea-maker. Other amenities include a recommended restaurant, and a sauna and jacuzzi. AA**. York is renowned for its many historical attractions, such as the Jorvik Viking Centre, the Castle Museum and the National Railway Museum, as well as a wealth of interesting shops. It is also an ideal touring centre for the North Yorkshire Moors and Dales.

£ *Minimum 2 nights dinner, bed and breakfast from £75. All year.*

MIDDLETHORPE HALL HOTEL
Bishopthorpe Road, York YO2 1QB
0904 641241

Only one and a half miles from the centre of the historic city of York and overlooking York racecourse, this fine William III country house has been sympathetically restored and is now a luxurious hotel. Elegant guest rooms have been equipped with modern conveniences, including private bathroom, colour television and direct-dial telephone. In the panelled dining room guests can enjoy superlative traditional cuisine, accompanied by an interesting selection of fine wines. This is an ideal base for touring York, the beautiful North York Moors and the many places of interest in the area.

£ *Based on 2 persons sharing double or twin room: from £78 per person per night (minimum 2 nights) for English breakfast, dinner and champagne on arrival.* ☐ *1 November to 30 April 1991.*

PAULEDA HOUSE HOTEL
123 Clifton, York YO3 6BL
0904 634745

Your hosts Freda and Paul offer you a warm welcome to the friendly and relaxed atmosphere of this small, comfortable hotel situated within the city boundary, less than one mile from York Minster and other attractions of this beautiful and historic city. All rooms have shower, toilet etc, colour TV, direct-dial telephone, hairdryer etc, and some rooms have four-poster beds. Special short breaks include wine with your first evening meal. Car parking available. Open all year.

£ *Bed, breakfast and evening dinner from £25 per person per night (minimum 2 nights).* ☐ *November 1990 to May 1991. From June to October 1991 from £30. Excludes all Bank Holidays. Christmas Breaks also available.*

SHIP INN
Acaster Malbis, York YO2 1XB
0904 705609

A picturesque holiday retreat on the banks of the Yorkshire Ouse. Situated just 3½ miles from historic York with its many attractions, the Ship Inn is ideal for holidaymakers and business people alike. 8 bedrooms, all with private facilities. Yorkshire Tourist Board registered. Excellent meals are served in the relaxed atmosphere of the old world Restaurant, and a wide range of lunches and evening snacks can be enjoyed in the friendly Riverside Bar adjacent to the garden. The inn has its own moorings for residents and visitors, and there is fishing nearby.

£ *Dinner, bed and breakfast: any two nights from £50.*
☐ *November to March, excluding Christmas.*

THE HILL HOTEL
60 York Road, Acomb, York YO2 5LW
0904 790777

The Hill Hotel is a beautiful Georgian building standing in 1½ acres of its own grounds. BTA commended, Egon Ronay, AA. Its 10 bedrooms (some with four posters) are all well equipped with colour television, radio, telephone, hairdryers, and tea and coffee making facilities. The hotel also has its own bar and car park. It is well placed for touring the Vale of York and surrounding area, being only 1½ miles from the city walls, two miles from York Minster and Jorvik Viking Centre, and 14 miles from Castle Howard.

£ *£75 for any two nights dinner, bed and breakfast.*

112   North Yorkshire

West Yorkshire

PARKWAY HOTEL
Otley Road, Leeds LS16 8AG
0532 672551

A neo-Tudor country house hotel in two acres of grounds. The hotel's leisurely charm and excellent restaurants will be appreciated. It is an ideal centre for touring Ilkley Moor, the nearby Yorkshire Dales, and for visiting Leeds, Harrogate and Bradford. Saturday night dinner/dances are held between September and May. Leisure complex, including pool, saunas, solarium, whirlpool, steam room, beauty salon, tennis courts, snooker room, gym. RAC, AA***.

£ *Dinner, bed and breakfast two consecutive nights (must include Friday, Saturday or Sunday night). From £36.00.* *All year.*

CHEVIN LODGE HOTEL
Yorkgate, Otley LS21 3NU
0943 467818

In the heart of "Emmerdale Farm" country, this AA and RAC*** luxury hotel is set in 50 acres of woodland and is convenient for visiting York, Harrogate and the Yorkshire Dales. Meals are taken in our renowned lakeside restaurant, where only finest fresh market produce is used. Vegetarians are welcome and well catered for. All rooms are en suite, with colour TV, in-house video, direct-dial telephone and beverage making facilities. Egon Ronay recommended.

£ *£89.00 per person for 2 nights dinner, bed and breakfast (Friday, Saturday, Sunday only). One extra night may be added pro rata.* *All year.*

HOLIDAY ACCOMMODATION
Classification Schemes in
England, Scotland and Wales

The National Tourist Boards for England, Scotland and Wales have agreed a common 'Crown Classification' scheme for **serviced (Board)** accommodation. All establishments are inspected regularly and are given a classification indicating their level of facilities and services.
There are six grades ranging from 'Listed' to 'Five Crowns' ♕♕♕♕♕'. The higher the classification, the more facilities and services offered. Crown classification is a measure of *facilities* not *quality*. A common quality grading scheme grades the quality of establishments as 'Approved', 'Commended' or 'Highly Commended' according to the accommodation, welcome and service they provide.
For **Self-Catering**, holiday homes in England are awarded 'Keys' after inspection and can also be 'Approved', 'Commended' or 'Highly Commended' according to the facilities available. In Scotland the Crown scheme includes self-catering accommodation and Wales also has a voluntary inspection scheme for self-catering grading from '1 (Standard)' to '5 (Excellent)'.
Caravan and Camping Parks can participate in the British Holiday Parks grading scheme from 'Approved (√)' to 'Excellent (√ √ √ √ √)'. In addition, each National Tourist Board has an annual award for high-quality caravan accommodation: in England – Rose Awards; in Scotland – Thistle Commendations; in Wales – Dragon Awards.
When advertisers supply us with the information, FHG Publications show Crowns and other awards or gradings, including AA, RAC, Egon Ronay etc. We also award a small number of Farm Holiday Guide Diplomas every year, based on readers' recommendations.

The pleasant village of Tintern lies by the River Wye, Gwent.

WALES

Spectacular mountain scenery, uncrowded coastal resorts, splendid historical treasures – if this attracts you then a holiday in Wales will more than meet your demands. In the south, the regions of Glamorgan and Gwent may be better known for their heavy industry, but they have a great deal to offer the holidaymaker. The coastline boasts a variety of popular resorts, while towards the border region, a great many castles, dating from Norman times, can still be seen. The lovely old border town of Monmouth delights visitors with its attractive Tudor and Georgian buildings set in old winding streets, while further south are the magnificent Roman ruins of Caerleon and the picturesque village of Tintern.

But the real heartland of Wales lies in the central and western regions. Here the visitor can relax in the magnificent countryside of Dyfed and Powys where local traditions thrive and the Welsh language is still spoken. This is a land with a splendid coastline while inland the remote hills and mountains provide memorable scenery, not least of which is the famous tourist attraction of the Brecon Beacons National Park with its magnificent and varied scenery. It's ideal countryside for the walker and wildlife enthusiast. Over to the west the superb coastline of Pembrokeshire with its dramatic headlands and sheltered coves has been designated a National Park.

But those with a taste for the dramatic will be more at home in the exhilarating scenery of the North, among the craggy peaks and cascading waterfalls, hidden lakes and wooded valleys of Snowdonia, while on the Island of Anglesey the visitor meets with a total contrast in the only really flat part of Wales. Here, among the stone-walled villages, the pace is slow and the atmosphere warm and friendly.

The Dee and Clwyd valleys offer abundant fishing waters surrounded by lovely abbeys and castles, and if you fancy something out of the ordinary, spend some time at the picturesque town of Portmeiron modelled on the beautiful Italian town of Portofino.

For further information contact the **Wales Tourist Board, Brunel House, Cardiff CF2 1UY (0222 499909)** or at the following addresses:

For North Wales (Clwyd, part-Gwynedd): **Wales Tourist Board, North Wales Regional Office, 77 Conway Road, Colwyn Bay, Clwyd LL29 7LN (0492 531731).**

For Mid Wales (Powys, part-Gwynedd, part-Dyfed): **Wales Tourist Board, Mid Wales Regional Office, Canolfan Owain Glyndwr, Machynlleth, Powys SY20 8EE (0654 2401).**

For South Wales (part-Dyfed, West, South and Mid Glamorgan, Gwent): **Wales Tourist Board, South Wales Regional Office, Ty Croeso, Gloucester Place, Swansea, West Glamorgan SA1 1TY (0792 465204).**

Clwyd

ALWYN HOUSE HOTEL
4 Upper Promenade, Colwyn Bay LL28 4BS
0492 532004

This delightful small hotel (formerly the Southlea) offers rest, comfort and a friendly welcome. All bedrooms are centrally heated, with washbasins, colour TV, tea/coffee making facilities, radio, baby-listening intercom and shaver points. There is a colour TV lounge and a beamed dining room. Highly recommended. Open all year. AA Listed. The hotel is ideal for touring Snowdonia National Park, Betws-y-Coed and Conwy Castle; close to Colwyn Bay's beach, shops, entertainment and sports facilities, including a dry-ski slope.

£ *Details of Spring and Autumn Breaks and Christmas/New Year bookings on request.*

ASHMOUNT HOTEL
Rhos-on-Sea, Colwyn Bay
0492 45479

Ashmount Hotel is detached, and beautifully situated on a quiet road close to the promenade. AA**, RAC**. Bedrooms are comfortable, all with shower/bathrooms en suite, TV with video channel, telephone, and tea and coffee making facilities. Ground floor bedrooms suitable for disabled. Residential licence. The elegant restaurant offers home cooking using fresh local produce. Local amenities include golf, squash, fishing, and a bowling green and leisure centre. Ideally situated for exploring North Wales.

£ *£27.90 per person per night for dinner, bed and breakfast. Minimum two nights.* ✪ *October to March excluding Christmas.*

EXPLANATION OF SYMBOLS

TA	Travel Agency Commission
♛	Number of Crowns
⚿	Number of Keys
🐕	Pets Welcome
🪆	Reductions for Children
♿	Suitable for Disabled
✪	Christmas Breaks

ABBEY GRANGE HOTEL
Llangollen LL20 8NN
0978 860753

Resting at the foot of the spectacular Horseshoe Pass with magnificent views to all sides, this family-run hotel offers an idyllic setting for your holiday, combining the character of an old country house with the comfort of modern amenities. The eight spacious bedrooms are all en suite, with colour TV, tea/coffee facilities and central heating. Catering is of a high standard, ranging from a comprehensive bar menu to full à la carte meals. Outside there is a spacious sun terrace and a large lawn. Pets are welcome by arrangement.

£ **£49 per person for 2 nights dinner, bed and breakfast; £60 per person for 2 days full board.** 1st October 1990 to 31st March 1991 (excluding Christmas and New Year).

THE HAWK AND BUCKLE INN
Llannefydd, Near Denbigh LL16 5ED
074-579 249

Every 20th century comfort is to be found at this welcoming seventeenth century village inn. All the en suite guest rooms in the tasteful extensions are equipped with telephones, tea/coffee making facilities and television; trouser press and hairdryer available. Egon Ronay, Ashley Courtenay. Furnishings are comfortable and pleasing to the eye. Local game, pork, lamb and freshly caught salmon and trout are imaginatively served in the Inn's popular restaurant, and varied and substantial bar snacks are offered at lunchtime. Hosts Robert and Barbara Pearson will happily supply a wealth of information on the area. Visa and Access accepted.

£ **£60 per person for 2 nights dinner, bed and breakfast, based on 2 persons sharing.** All year.

Other specialised
FHG PUBLICATIONS

* Recommended COUNTRY HOTELS OF BRITAIN   £2.99

* Recommended WAYSIDE INNS OF BRITAIN   £2.99

* PETS WELCOME!   £2.50

* BED AND BREAKFAST IN BRITAIN   £1.99

Published annually. Please add 50p postage (U.K. only) when ordering from the publishers:

**FHG PUBLICATIONS LTD
Abbey Mill Business Centre, Seedhill,
Paisley, Renfrewshire PA1 1JN**

Clwyd 117

Dyfed

HIGHCLIFFE HOTEL
Aberporth, Cardigan
0239 810534

A friendly, 15-bedroomed family hotel with bar, restaurant, lounge and Sky TV lounge. AA**, RAC**. Bedrooms and family rooms are comfortable, and some overlook the wide sweep of Cardigan Bay. You are only 150 yards from two safe, sandy beaches. Guests will receive a warm welcome and the best of personal attention at all times, and the quiet and pleasant atmosphere will ensure that they have a peaceful and relaxing stay. Golf, fishing, sailing, riding and pony trekking are available nearby, and this is an excellent base from which to tour West Wales.

[£] **£29.50 per person per night for dinner, bed and breakfast. Minimum stay two nights.** ☐ *All year.*

BEGGARS REACH HOTEL
Burton, Milford Haven SA73 1PD
0646 600700

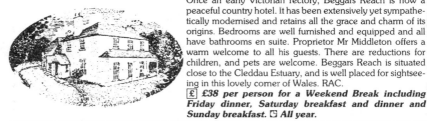

Once an early Victorian rectory, Beggars Reach is now a peaceful country hotel. It has been extensively yet sympathetically modernised and retains all the grace and charm of its origins. Bedrooms are well furnished and equipped and all have bathrooms en suite. Proprietor Mr Middleton offers a warm welcome to all his guests. There are reductions for children, and pets are welcome. Beggars Reach is situated close to the Cleddau Estuary, and is well placed for sightseeing in this lovely corner of Wales. RAC.

[£] **£38 per person for a Weekend Break including Friday dinner, Saturday breakfast and dinner and Sunday breakfast.** ☐ *All year.*

TREGYNON COUNTRY FARMHOUSE HOTEL
Gwaun Valley, Near Fishguard SA65 9TU
0239 820531

Escape to a different world. Wales' award-winning family run 16th century licensed Farm Hotel nestles in foothills of Preseli mountains with magnificent views over Gwaun Valley. Own ancient forest, Iron-age fort, waterfall. Abundant wildlife with mountain walks and mile-long sweep of Newport sands close at hand. RAC acclaimed, winner of Pembrokeshire Coast National Park Award. Renowned and imaginative cuisine as featured in "Here's Health" and "The Vegetarian", using fresh produce whenever possible — including own trout. Log fires in winter. WTB Commended, Ashley Courtenay Recommended.

[£] **From £52 for 2 nights dinner, bed and breakfast.** ☐ *1 November to 21 March (excluding Christmas & New Year).*

ROYAL OAK
Rhandirmwyn, Llandovery SA20 0NY
055-06 201

The proprietors of this delightful inn have managed to combine informality with efficiency, friendliness and courteous good service. AA Listed, Les Routiers. Spacious rooms offer comfort as well as attractive decor, and most have colour television and private facilities. The very full menu presented in the restaurant caters for most tastes, and bar snacks are available together with a range of local beers. Visa and Access accepted.

£ *Reductions for groups and for stays of four nights or more.* ☐ *Open all year.*

COACH HOUSE INN
116 Main Street, Pembroke SA71 4HN
0646 684602

The Coach House, situated in the main street of the historic town of Pembroke offers a very warm welcome to the many visitors who come to this beautiful part of Wales. It is ideally situated for exploring the spectacular coast with its many sandy beaches, wonderful walks and wildlife. All bedrooms have en suite bathrooms, colour television, direct-dial telephone and tea/coffee facilities. The Horseshoe Grill provides an excellent choice of dishes, using mainly local produce, and bar meals are served in the attractive bar.

£ *Minimum 2 nights stay £55 per person for dinner, bed and breakfast.* ☐ *All year.*

WAUNIFOR
Maesycrugiau, Pencander SA39 9LX
055-935 280/430 Fax: 055-935 304

[TA]

Family-run stone cottages and flats near the Teifi River, West Wales. Sleep 2-12; colour television and some open fires. Amenities include heated and covered outdoor swimming pool (Easter to end October), table tennis, pool table, launderette, off-licence. Excellent pub food and licensed restaurants nearby. Local game fishing, riding (indoor school), trekking. Near mountains, rivers, forests, moors – ideal for rambling, touring, birdwatching (buzzards, red kites, occasional ospreys, redstarts etc). Just half an hour's drive to coast with sandy coves and rocky cliffs. Free brochure.

£ *Winter: for 2 persons: 2 nights £45 including VAT, linen and fuel. Extra nights/people sharing – cheaper rates. Special Christmas and New Year breaks.* ☐ *Open all year, but short breaks not normally available Easter, Whitsun or Summer Holidays.*

LOCHMEYLER FARM
Pen-y-cwm, Near Solva SA62 6LL
0348 837724/837705

Lochmeyler is a 220-acre dairy farm, situated in the centre of St. David's Peninsula. The 11th century farmhouse has been modernised but still retains its olde worlde character, with beams, and open fires early and late season. En suite bedrooms have colour TV, video, tea-making facilities, hair dryers etc, and some rooms have four-poster beds. There are two lounges (one for smokers) and a spacious dining room offering a choice of menu, vegetarian as well as traditional farmhouse. There is plenty of wildlife, with farm trails, ponds and streams. Children over 10 are welcome. AA QQQ, RAC Highly Acclaimed.
☐ *All year.*

Dyfed

RAMSEY HOUSE
Lower Moor, St. David's SA62 6RP
0437 720321

Pamper yourselves with a Leisure Break at Ramsey House, the ideal location for touring in unspoiled Pembrokeshire, only half a mile from the spectacular coastal path and 12th century cathedral. Just come to relax and enjoy our Welsh speciality cooking, or join one of our Car Treasure Hunt weekends, to explore the hidden haunts of Pembrokeshire. Microwave Cookery weekends also arranged to help you make the most of your microwave. Licensed bar. Open all year. Dogs welcome. Parking. AA/RAC Listed.
£ *Any 2 or more nights dinner, bed and breakfast £21.50 per person per night. October to March (excluding Christmas and New Year).*

Glamorgan

ANGEL HOTEL
Castle Street, Cardiff CF1 2QZ
0222 232633 Fax: 0222 396212

Cardiff's premier hotel, situated in the centre of the Welsh capital, overlooking Cardiff Castle and Cardiff Arms Park. Skilfully refurbished to blend elegance and service with quiet efficiency. RAC****. All the luxurious bedrooms and suites have private bathrooms, direct-dial telephone, remote control colour TV, tea/coffee facilities etc. The most attractive restaurant offers a wide selection of skilfully prepared dishes. The Leisure Club incorporates the most up-to-date exercise equipment, sauna and solarium. Cardiff is an ideal centre for exploring Welsh culture and heritage.
£ *Bed and full Welsh breakfast £36.50 per person per night; dinner, bed and breakfast £51.50. Murder Mystery Weekends — details on request. Fri/Sat/Sun all year.*

PUBLISHER'S NOTE

While every effort is made to ensure accuracy, we regret that FHG Publications cannot accept responsibility for errors, omissions or misrepresentation in our entries or any consequences thereof. Prices in particular should be checked because we go to press early. We will follow up complaints but cannot act as arbiters or agents for either party.

Gwent

THE CELTIC MANOR HOTEL
Coldra Woods, Newport NP6 2YA
0633 413000

Take a well-deserved break in the luxurious comfort of Wales' finest hotel. A range of air-conditioned bedrooms, including four-posters and unique suites, have been designed and appointed to extremely high standards. AA/RAC****, Egon Ronay. The hotel boasts two of the region's finest restaurants, under the expert guidance of Trefor Jones, Welsh Chef of the Year 1989. The hotel's superb leisure facilities are freely available for guests to enjoy, including an indoor heated pool, sauna and gymnasium. There are many places of interest to explore locally, and this is an ideal centre for touring.
£ **£55 single room, £75 double/twin room for dinner, bed and breakfast. Friday, Saturday or Sunday; or any Thursday and Friday or Sunday and Monday 2 night stay.** All year except New Year.

WEST USK LIGHTHOUSE
St Brides, Near Newport NP1 9SF
0633 810126/815582

Unique opportunity to stay in a 170-year-old lighthouse, recently converted into a wonderful guest house. All rooms wedge-shaped and equipped with colour TV, satellite/video link, and tea/coffee making facilities. Ideal for bird watching, fishing and golf. Walks along deserted seashore to nearest pub/restaurant. Relaxation floating — the ultimate in deep relaxation — and champagne breakfast are optional extras. Only 10 minutes from Junction 28 of M4 and half an hour's drive from Cardiff. Definitely lots to do and see — an experience not to be missed.
£ **£36 for a double room en suite for bed and breakfast for 2; (£55 including champagne breakfast); £18 single.** All year.

John Carter suggests . . .
GWENT — BORDER COUNTY

Nestling in the south-east corner of Wales, Gwent is an undulating county which includes the ever popular Wye Valley. Other attractions are Chepstow, Abergavenny, Tintern Forest and Tredegar.

Gwynedd

TREFEDDIAN HOTEL
Aberdovey LL35 0SB
065-472 213

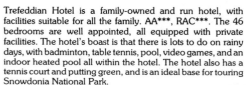

Trefeddian Hotel is a family-owned and run hotel, with facilities suitable for all the family. AA***, RAC***. The 46 bedrooms are well appointed, all equipped with private facilities. The hotel's boast is that there is lots to do on rainy days, with badminton, table tennis, pool, video games, and an indoor heated pool all within the hotel. The hotel also has a tennis court and putting green, and is an ideal base for touring Snowdonia National Park.

£ *From £34 per person per night for half board, inclusive of VAT. Weekly rates also available.* ⌸ *23 March 1991 to 2 January 1992.*

BRYN BRAS
—CASTLE—

Llanrug, Near Caernarfon
Gwynedd LL55 4RE
Tel: 0286 870210

Welcome to beautiful Bryn Bras Castle – tasteful Castle Apartments, Tower House and Mini-Cottage for 2-6 within unique, romantic, turreted Regency Castle. Centrally situated amidst breathtaking scenery for enjoying North Wales' magnificent mountains, beaches, heritage and history. Many local restaurant and inns. Each apartment is fully self-contained, gracious, clean, with idyllically individual character. Comfortable furnishings, generously equipped – dishwasher, microwave. Free central heating, hot water, duvets/bed linen.

ALL HIGHEST WTB GRADE (except one)

32 acres of landscaped gardens, woods, panoramic hill walks overlooking the sea, Anglesey, Mount Snowdon. The comfortable, warm and welcoming Castle in truly peaceful surroundings is always open.

Brochure sent with pleasure. End September to mid-May: 2 nights for 2/6 persons, per apartment £55-£145.

BRON EIFION
Rhyd Ddu, Beddgelert

Attractive semi-detached house available for self-catering holidays on the edge of a small village at the foot of Snowdon. There are splendid mountain, valley and pass walks from the village (including path up Snowdon), and it is an excellent centre for riding, fishing and touring. The well-equipped accommodation comprises three bedrooms, two living rooms, bathroom and modern kitchen. Fridge, airing cupboard, heaters; cot available. The property enjoys superb mountain views, and there is a terrace and rough garden. Shop and inn (serving meals) nearby. Sorry, no pets. Apply: **Davies, 218 Clive Road, London SE21 8BS (081-670 2756).**
£ *Short breaks by arrangement outside main holiday period.*

BRYN BRAS CASTLE [TA]
Llanrug, Near Caernarfon LL55 4RE
0286 870210

Welcome to beautiful Bryn Bras Castle, tasteful castle apartments, Tower House and mini-cottage in unique, romantic, turreted Regency castle (Grade II* listed building). Set amidst breathtaking scenery with easy access to North Wales' superb beaches. Each fully self-contained apartment has individual character and comfortable furnishings. Generous range of appliances – dishwasher, microwave. Free central heating, hot water, linen. Truly peaceful surroundings – 32 acres of landscaped gardens, woodland walks; views. **ALL BUT ONE WTB HIGHEST GRADE.** Open all year. Brochure sent with pleasure.
£ *SELF CATERING – per apartment for 2/6 persons: 2 nights from £55-£145.* End September to mid-May.

CHOCOLATE HOUSE   [TA]
Plas Treflan, Caeathro, Caernarfon LL55 2SE
0286 4872

The Chocolate House is just made for couples. You stay in a personal mini-cottage with free choice from à la carte and vegetarian menu and meals for two. AA*. There is a separate bar with a splendid selection of malts, cognacs and clarets. Other amenities include colour television, videos, badminton, tennis, a camera darkroom, snooker and a solarium. Visa and Access accepted.

£ *All inclusive short breaks from £25 per person per day.*

GORFFWYSFA HOTEL
St David's Road, Caernarvon LL55 1BH
0286 2647

Gorffwysfa is a Victorian licensed hotel in a superior area of Caernarvon enjoying magnificent sea and country views. The many ornate period features blend well with the most modern amenities, so providing a high standard of comfort and relaxation in spacious surroundings. Some rooms with en suite facilities and some with sea views; all are well furnished, with central heating, colour TV, clock radio and drinks facilities. Ideal for touring — fine beaches, historic buildings and sporting facilities. Fishing, golf and pony trekking breaks can be arranged.

£ *Bed and breakfast from £12.00 per person per night. Special breaks October to March £37 per person for 2 nights dinner, bed and breakfast.*

Gwynedd 123

TAN DINAS
Llanddeiniolen, Caernarvon LL55 3AR
0248 670098

A modernised stone farmhouse situated in a secluded yet central location, with a pleasant garden sloping down to a small stream. There is a colour TV lounge and a separate dining room for guests. Children are welcome, and a cot, high chair and babysitting are available. The area is ideal for touring, also all types of fishing, walking and pony trekking. Caernarvon, Bangor, Anglesey and Snowdon all within easy reach. Open April to October with central heating and open fires. Tourist Board Listed.

£ *Bed and breakfast £11 per night; bed, breakfast and evening meal £14.* ⌂ *April to October.*

SUNNYBANKS GUEST HOUSE
Llanrwst Road, Conwy LL32 8LT
0492 593845

Set in a beautiful garden, this pretty little guest house is set off the main road and overlooking Conwy Castle. Sunnybanks has seven cosy bedrooms with TVs and beverage making facilities. Residential licence; TV lounge and board games for amusement in rainy weather. Conwy is the gem of Welsh history, set in the heart of Aberconwy between the mountains and the sea, and boasts a wealth of exciting activities to appeal to all interests, including walking, mountaineering, golf, bowls, tennis, fishing, riding, and sailing

£ *From £30 per person for two nights dinner, bed and breakfast.* ⌂ *30 September to 31 March. Special Christmas breaks.*

BRON EIFION COUNTRY HOUSE HOTEL
Criccieth LL52 0SA
0766 522385

This gracious and comfortable house, a 120-year-old gentleman's residence, is situated in a lovely country estate, close to Snowdonia National Park and only half a mile from the popular seaside resort of Criccieth. AA/RAC***. All the individually furnished bedrooms have private bath/shower, colour TV, clock radio, telephone and tea/coffee making facilities. Local leisure amenities include golf, shooting, water sports, tennis and clay-pigeon shooting; clock golf and croquet may be played in the hotel gardens. Ideal for exploring the many places of interest in this delightful part of Wales.

£ *Dinner, bed and breakfast from £33. Special weekly rates and Christmas package.*

CLIFTON HOUSE HOTEL
Smithfield Square, Dolgellau LL40 1ES
0341 422554

A well appointed, centrally situated town house hotel, personally run by the proprietors Rob and Pauline Dix. All bedrooms have tea/coffee facilities, colour TV and hairdryer; most are en suite. AA/RAC*. Pauline's cooking, using fresh local produce, is popular with locals and visitors alike, and has gained "Taste of Wales" recognition for the comfortable Cellar Restaurant. This part of southern Snowdonia is ideal for walking, with pony trekking, fishing, golf and dry-slope skiing all nearby. The Clifton is the ideal base for exploring this undiscovered part of Wales.

£ *£60 per person for 2 nights dinner, bed and breakfast with en suite facilities (£52 without). Based on 2 persons sharing.*
⌂ *1st October up to Easter except Christmas and New Year.*

124 *Gwynedd*

BULL HOTEL
London Road, Valley, Near Holyhead LL65 3DP
0407 740351

This friendly hotel is situated on the A5, only three and a half miles from the ferry to Ireland, and within easy reach of some of Britain's finest beaches. This is an ideal location for a wide range of outdoor activities, including fishing and golf (five courses on the island). Les Routiers recommended. RAC**. All 14 bedrooms have telephone, colour TV, and tea/coffee makers, and most have private bathrooms. In the evenings guests can enjoy the atmosphere of our "old world" bars and eating house, with rustic brick walls, checked table cloths and candlelight.

£ *2 nights dinner, bed and breakfast (double room) £45.00 per person.* All year.

TY MAWR HOTEL
Llanbedr LL45 2NH
034-123 440

Originally a 16th century farmhouse, Ty Mawr Hotel stands in its own lovely and flower-laden grounds within Snowdonia National Park. AA**, RAC**; BTA Recommended. There are 10 attractive bedrooms, all with en suite facilities. The restaurant, overlooking the garden, offers a wide choice of imaginative dishes at reasonable prices, complemented by a fine wine list, while the well-stocked bar offers tasty meals seven days a week. Good trout and salmon fishing can be had on the River Artro opposite, with bathing, sailing, riding, golf, and fine walking nearby.

£ *£68 per person for two nights dinner, bed and breakfast. £72 in July and August.* All year.

HEADLANDS HOTEL
Hill Terrace, Llandudno LL39 2LS
0492 77485

For sea and Snowdonia. This family run hotel has earned a reputation for high standards at reasonable prices. With direct access to cliff walks yet only five minutes to the town centre. Views over the bay and across the Conwy Estuary to the mountains of Snowdonia. AA**, RAC**. Ashley Courtenay, Les Routiers recommended. Excellent facilities and renowned cuisine. Most rooms have private baths and all have television, central heating, and teasmade, also radio and telephone. Some have four poster beds.

£ *From £20 per day bed and breakfast; from £25 per day dinner, bed and breakfast.* All year except January and February.

John Carter suggests . . .

The sheltered valley of the river Conwy has provided the perfect setting for one of Britain's finest gardens — Bodnant Garden, in the care of the National Trust. Just off the A470, 8 miles South of Llandudno, the colourful collection of rhododendrons, camellias and magnolias contrasts with the spectacular views of Snowdonia across the valley. Don't miss this experience if you're in the area between Easter and October.

Powys

VICTORIA WELLS FOREST CABIN HOLIDAY MOTEL
Powys

High in the verdant mountains of central Wales, situated in 24 acres of woodlands and with miles of natural parkland and riverside walks, Victoria Wells is the ideal holiday location for those who want to unwind and shed the tensions of modern living. Three-quarters-of-a mile of private fishing, heated swimming pool. Restaurant and bar. Horse riding and pony trekking centres nearby. All accommodation centrally heated, with en suite bathrooms, colour TV and tea/coffee making facilities. Arguably as like the Canadian Rockies as you will find in this country! Bookings: Victoria Wells Booking Office, Grosvenor House, 20 St Andrews Crescent, Cardiff CF1 3DD (0222 340558 Fax: 0222 223692).
£ *Bargain Breaks 3 days £55 for accommodation, full English breakfast and evening meal.* ☐ *January–December.*

LANSDOWNE HOTEL AND RESTAURANT
The Watton, Brecon LD3 7EG
0874 3321

This carefully restored Georgian building overlooks a small park, and is only a few minutes' walk from the town centre and all amenities. Personally supervised by the proprietors, great emphasis is placed on creating a warm, friendly atmosphere. Centrally heated throughout, the hotel offers 12 individually designed bedrooms en suite, all with colour TV, telephone, radio and tea/coffee making facilities. All tastes are catered for in the cosy restaurant, renowned locally for its excellent cuisine at reasonable prices. Two residents' lounges, one with colour TV, complete the hotel's amenities.
£ *From £60 per person for 2 nights dinner, bed and breakfast, inc. pre-dinner drink and special menu. Extra nights pro rata.* ☐ *All year.*

John Carter suggests . . .
POWYS — MOUNTAINOUS AND LANDLOCKED

With many border castles and the Brecon Beacons, which cover the south of the county, Powys can be very spectacular. You will also find the best stretches of Offa's Dyke, Hay-on-Wye, the steam railway at Llanfair Caereinion, Radnor Forest, the fortified house of Tretower, the farming centre at Builth Wells and the abandoned medieval town of Cefnllys.

THE BEACONS GUEST HOUSE
16 Bridge Street, Brecon LD3 8AH
0874 3339

Friendly atmosphere guaranteed at our Grade II Listed Georgian guest house. All rooms comfortably furnished, with beverage trays. Most en suite with colour TV. Private parking, cosy bar, spacious dining room and residents' lounge. Guests can enjoy our excellent home-cooked evening meals, prepared with fresh local produce and fresh vegetables from the garden. AA Listed, Taste of Wales Recommended. The Beacons is ideally located to explore the market town of Brecon, with its museums, Cathedral, pretty River Usk and canal. For the more adventurous, there are the Brecon Beacons and other local attractions.
£ *Bargain Breaks from £39.00. Please phone or write for brochure.*

ROCK PARK HOTEL AND ACTIVITY CENTRE
Llandrindod Wells LD1 6AE
0597 822021

The Rock Park Hotel is a rambling, comfortable old coaching inn, with the Victorian additions reflecting the heyday of Llandrindod Wells as an inland spa of considerable importance. Within the beautiful sheltered grounds are facilities for activities to keep all members of the family occupied: indoor heated pool, assault course, archery, pottery, croquet; canoeing, sailing, windsurfing on the lake; fishing and golf nearby; abseiling and climbing instruction. Accommodation varies from luxury bedrooms with en suite facilities to multi-bedded rooms for youngsters.
£ *Activity Breaks — special weekend programmes with qualified instruction and all equipment provided, from £89.* ☐ *Autumn, Spring, Winter, some in Summer.*

EXPLANATION OF SYMBOLS

TA	Travel Agency Commission
♛	Number of Crowns
⚷	Number of Keys
🐕	Pets Welcome
🎠	Reductions for Children
♿	Suitable for Disabled
🎄	Christmas Breaks

The symbols are arranged in the
same order throughout the book so that
looking down each page will give a quick comparison.

Powys 127

SCOTLAND

Arriving from the South at the Scottish Borders, the peaceful moorlands and rich green pastures contrast with the scars of its turbulent past – the ruined abbeys of Melrose, Jedburgh, Kelso and Dryburgh. These and other charming Border towns are all excellent bases from which to explore the splendid castles and romantic landscape which inspired Walter Scott.

Over to the West are the lush valleys of the Southern Lowlands, the soft hills around the Solway and the Ayrshire coast. This is the Burns country, where his birthplace, the humble thatched cottage at Alloway, can be visited. Inland towards southern Lanarkshire, the verdant hillsides of the Clyde valley lead down to Glasgow, Scotland's largest city whose rejuvenated Victorian charm and energy have created a fast-growing tourism centre.

To the East there's the national capital, Edinburgh, dominated by its spectacular castle and boasting all kinds of attractions for the visitor. Northwards the bridges over the river Forth carry you by road or rail to Fife (for the 'gowf' at St. Andrews?), to Dundee across the Tay and then further North and East to the granite city of Aberdeen.

But for most, the real Scotland begins at Stirling, Perth and Oban, gateways to the Highlands and Islands. Here the high peaks, the wild sea lochs and the wooded glens offer the least spoilt and most sparsely populated area of Great Britain.

The Edinburgh Festival (mid/late August) is probably the high spot of Scotland's entertainment year. Glasgow has its own 'Mayfest' in May and the National Gaelic Mod is usually in October. For something distinctly Scottish, however, try to spend at least part of a day at one of the many Highland Games held throughout Scotland in the late summer. You'll enjoy caber tossing, Highland dancing, athletics and pipe band competitions – often all at the same time!

For details of what's happening around Scotland, contact: **The Scottish Tourist Board, 23 Ravelston Terrace, Edinburgh EH4 3EU (031-332 2433).**

GOLF VIEW HOTEL
NAIRN

Renowned for its excellent cuisine and service the Golf View has something for everyone – heated outdoor pool, sauna, tennis, games and regular entertainment plus the Nairn Championship Golf Course on your doorstep. Colour TV, telephone etc, in all rooms.
Midweek, Weekend and 7 day breaks available.
Inclusive Midweek and Weekend Golf Holidays. Parties welcome.
For reservations and further details please phone:

Tel: (0667) 52301
Telex: 75134

Argyll

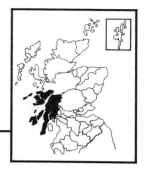

CAIRNDOW STAGECOACH INN
Cairndow PA26 8BN
049-96 286/252

[TA]

Situated on the upper reaches of Loch Fyne, this historic coaching inn affords magnificent views of the surrounding landscape. Just 15 minutes from Loch Lomond via the Arrochar Alps, an ideal centre for touring the Western Highlands and the Trossachs. The bedrooms, most of which are en suite, have telephones, electric blankets, shaver point, radio and baby listening. There is a beer garden and games room. For a real touch of luxury there is a sauna, solarium and exercise room. Please phone for brochure.
[£] *Two days dinner, bed and breakfast £50 per person. Leisure facilities included. Extra days pro rata.*
January to 20th May 1991; October-December.

CLACHAIG INN (Dept. FHG)
Glencoe PA39 4HX
08552 252

Clachaig is set amidst the magnificent mountains of historic Glencoe. Under family management, this ancient drovers' inn continues the tradition of a warm and friendly welcome and the best of Highland hospitality. With en suite bedrooms and Scottish home cooking, Clachaig is the perfect base from which to tour, sightsee and savour the atmosphere so special to the West Coast. Also ideal for walking, climbing, sailing, cycling etc. After a pleasant day out, what better than a delicious home-cooked meal and a relaxing drink in the friendly bars, with a selection of real ales and a choice of some fifty finest malt whiskies. **Good Beer Guide.**
[£] *Three day break dinner, bed and breakfast from £63.*
Open all year.

THE GIGHA HOTEL
Isle of Gigha
05835 254

Relax and unwind in the tranquil atmosphere of Gigha, the fairest isle in the Hebrides. The Gigha Hotel offers you a delightful stay, excellent international cuisine and a warm island welcome. Sample the Gigha Golf Club nine-hole course and take a break between holes to admire the magnificent views. Stroll along the sandy beaches, or visit the legendary gardens of Achamore. Gigha is only 20 minutes away from the mainland by car ferry from Tayinloan. Under new management. Ashley Courtenay, BHRCA.
[£] *3 nights dinner, bed and breakfast £42 per person per night. October to March. Christmas and New Year terms on request.*

STONEFIELD CASTLE HOTEL
Tarbert
0880 820836 Fax: 0880 820929

Peaceful tranquillity in the Mull of Kintyre at Stonefield Castle Hotel, set in 60 acres of beautiful private wooded gardens on the shores of Loch Fyne. AA and RAC***. This splendid and well maintained hotel has 33 bedrooms and suites with private bathroom, each reflecting the original dignity and elegance of the castle. The Egon Ronay recommended dining room is complemented by the panelled cocktail bar, two comfortable lounges, and inviting library. Outdoor swimming pool, tennis court, and putting green. Sailing, golf, pony trekking and fishing facilities nearby.

[£] **Two nights dinner, bed and breakfast from £28 per person per night.** 2 October to 30 April.

Ayrshire

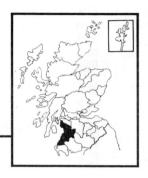

BUSBIEHILL GUEST HOUSE
Knockentiber, Kilmarnock KA2 9AJ
0563 32985

This homely country guest house is situated in the heart of Burns country and is convenient for touring Loch Lomond, the Trossachs, Edinburgh and the Clyde Coast. There are many fine golf courses in the area, and other outdoor activities can be arranged. The comfortable accommodation includes single rooms, double rooms with bathroom and family suites, all with tea-making facilities. Children are welcome — cot, high chair, babysitting, pony rides and swings are available. A car is essential — ample parking space. Open all year. Licensed.

[£] **Bed and breakfast from £8.50 per person, evening meal £4.**

HOSPITALITY INN
46 Annick Road,
Irvine KA11 4LD
Telephone: 0294 74272

RAC AA ★★★★   STB Commended

Enjoy a "Highlife" value break Luxury Weekend
* All rooms en suite with luxury facilities
* Leisure amenities including fun pool with chute, jacuzzi, putting green, 9-hole golf course, football pitch ready 1992
* Ideal for touring Burns' Country, Culzean Castle, etc.
* Many fine golf courses in the area
* Christmas and New Year Packages

One of 20 Mount Charlotte Thistle Hotels in Scotland which offer Short Break Holidays.

Banffshire

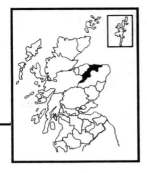

THE HIGHLAND HAVEN
Shore Street, Macduff
0261 32408

An attractive hotel overlooking the harbour in the picturesque fishing village of Macduff. AA***. Those venturing north will find themselves amply rewarded — picturesque coastline, quaint harbour, local heritage, golfing, fishing and the warmest of Scottish welcomes from proprietors Bill and Eleanor Alcock. Bedrooms are comfortable and well appointed — all are en suite — and good food is served by a friendly and courteous staff. Ample leisure facilities include spa bath, Turkish steam room, sauna and snooker. Near the famous whisky and castle trails.
[£] *From £50 per person for two nights dinner, bed and breakfast.* ⌾ *1 September to 31 May. Summer breaks (20% extra) also available.*

FOR THE MUTUAL GUIDANCE OF GUEST AND HOST

Every year literally thousands of holidays, short-breaks and overnight stops are arranged through our guides, the vast majority without any problems at all. In a handful of cases, however, difficulties do arise about bookings, which often could have been prevented from the outset.

It is important to remember that when accommodation has been booked, both parties — guests and hosts — have entered into a form of contract. We hope that the following points will provide helpful guidance.

GUESTS: When enquiring about accommodation, be as precise as possible. Give exact dates, numbers in your party and the ages of any children. State the number and type of rooms wanted and also what catering you require — bed and breakfast, full board, etc. Make sure that the position about evening meals is clear — and about pets, reductions for children or any other special points.

Read our reviews carefully to ensure that the proprietors you are going to contact can supply what you want. Ask for a letter confirming all arrangements, if possible.

If you have to cancel, do so as soon as possible. Proprietors do have the right to retain deposits and under certain circumstances to charge for cancelled holidays if adequate notice is not given and they cannot re-let the accommodation.

HOSTS: Give details about your facilities and about any special conditions. Explain your deposit system clearly and arrangements for cancellations, charges, etc, and whether or not your terms include VAT.

If for any reason you are unable to fulfill an agreed booking without adequate notice, you may be under an obligation to arrange alternative suitable accommodation or to make some form of compensation.

While every effort is made to ensure accuracy, we regret that FHG Publications cannot accept responsibility for errors, omissions or misrepresentation in our entries or any consequences thereof. Prices in particular should be checked because we go to press early. We will follow up complaints but cannot act as arbiters or agents for either party.

Short Break Attractions in
EDINBURGH – Capital of Scotland

Edinburgh, one of the world's most beautiful capital cities, offers the visitor a truly unique experience. Built on a series of spectacular hills and valleys, Edinburgh is a gracious city, famed for the elegance of its classical architecture, dramatic skylines, panoramic views, parks and open spaces.

Steeped in history, Edinburgh is nevertheless a modern city, bustling with activity. Its friendly citizens delight in answering questions about their city. The visitor, constantly discovering something new to savour, inevitably grows to love this queen of cities. You may leave, but one day your memories will draw you back.

The Capital of Scotland since the 12th century, Edinburgh can trace her origins to the 5th century. Dominating the city skyline is the world-famous Castle, standing proudly on its soaring rock, testament to Edinburgh's leading role in Scottish history.

The fascinating Royal Mile, the bustling street that is the heart of Edinburgh's medieval Old Town, runs downhill from the Castle to the Palace of Holyroodhouse. Throughout its length, numerous picturesque wynds and closes are a living link with a bygone age.

Immediately to the north of the Old Town, on the far side of the valley, lie Princes Street and the eighteenth-century New Town. Here the visitor can explore Edinburgh's Georgian architectural splendour, in the form of classical buildings, tree-lined squares and crescents, linked by wide and handsome streets.

The major event of the year is undoubtedly the Edinburgh International Festival. During the last three weeks in August, with a different theme each year, Edinburgh hosts music, opera, ballet and theatrical performances from all over the world.

The famous Fringe runs parallel to the

Holyrood Palace

Princes Street

official Festival and gives an opportunity to hundreds of new theatrical and artistic talents to perform before an international audience. The Military Tattoo brings the Old Town to a standstill with a nightly performance (except Sundays) for three weeks of military music and displays from all over the world. At the same time the Edinburgh International Film Festival launches its programme for film buffs. And the Jazz Festival sets the town booming.

Outwith this three-week period, however, Edinburgh does not sleep. The early months of the year bring the international rugby matches to Murrayfield Stadium, notably the five nations' tournament. Spring opens with the Folk Festival in the month of March. June summons Scotland's farmers to the Capital with the Royal Highland Show at Ingliston – good day out for all. Autumn is a splendid time to visit the city, after the rush of the Festival has passed and the leaves turn a golden hue.

The festive season brings an air of excitement to the city, Christmas shopping in Princes Street takes on fresh meaning. And why not come and celebrate 'Hogmanay' the New Year, in Scotland's Capital?

For further information contact: **Edinburgh Tourist Centre, Waverley Market, 3 Princes Street, Edinburgh EH2 2QP. Telephone: 031-557 1700 Telex: 727143 Fax: 031-557 5118.**

Scotland 133

Edinburgh & Lothians

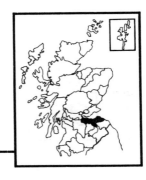

REDHEUGH HOTEL
Bayswell Park, Dunbar EH42 1AE
0368 62793

Commended

The Redheugh Hotel is situated in a quiet, residential area, only 5 minutes' walk from the town centre and the railway station. All bedrooms have central heating, colour TV, radio, direct-dial telephone, tea/coffee facilities, mini-bar and private bathroom with shower. AA/RAC**. Guests can relax in the comfortable residents' lounge while their choice from the extensive menu is prepared from fresh local produce. This is superb golfing country, with 14 courses in the area including the famous Muirfield. Golf packages can be arranged, also sea and river fishing. A warm welcome awaits you from Janette and Peter.
[£] *Dinner, bed and breakfast from £27.50 per person (1 October to 30 April), from £33.00 (1 May to 30 September). Minimum 2 nights, sharing double/twin room.*

DALMAHOY HOTEL, GOLF AND COUNTRY CLUB
Kirknewton EH27 8EB
031-333 1845

This imposing Georgian mansion, Country Club Hotels' newest property, is situated in 1000 acres of beautiful countryside at the foot of the Pentland Hills. Seven miles from Edinburgh, it is an international golf and leisure resort of the highest calibre. The improved famous golf courses are even more challenging, and for the non-golfer the excellent leisure facilities offer a refreshing swim, sauna and steam room, fitness studio, squash and tennis courts. Country Club Hotels offer first class accommodation in some of Britain's most attractive countryside.
[£] *From £40 per person dinner, bed and breakfast, minimum 2 nights. Golf breaks from £140 per person. Single supplement £15.* All year.

Available from most bookshops, the 1991 edition of THE GOLF GUIDE covers details of every UK golf course – well over 2000 entries – for holiday or business golf. Hundreds of hotel entries offer convenient accommodation, accompanying details of the courses – the 'pro', par score, length etc.
Old Thorns Golf Course & Hotel, Hampshire, features on the front cover with golfing editorial from the Professional Golfers' Association who also endorse the guide.
£5.99 from bookshops or £6.50 including postage from FHG Publications, Abbey Mill Business Centre, Paisley PA1 1JN.

Fife

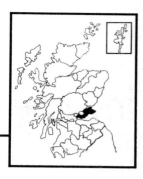

ACTIVITY AND LEISURE HOLIDAYS IN
THE KINGDOM OF FIFE
FIFE OFFERS A SUPERB RANGE OF INDOOR AND OUTDOOR LEISURE FACILITIES INCLUDING GOLF, FISHING, CURLING, ICE-SKATING, BOWLING, CARPET BOWLS, TEN-PIN BOWLING, SWIMMING, WIND-SURFING, SAILING, RIDING, HILL WALKING AND MUCH MORE. OR JUST ENJOY THE BEAUTIFUL COUNTRYSIDE, MILES OF GOLDEN BEACHES AND CHARMING FISHING VILLAGES.

Free colour brochure – Ring 0592 756684 or write to Glenrothes Tourist Promotions Ltd., Department RSB, Glenrothes House, North Street, Glenrothes, Fife, KY7 5PB.

FERNIE CASTLE HOTEL
Letham, Near Cupar KY7 7RU
033-781 381 Fax: 033-781 422

Fernie Castle is a small luxury hotel specialising in the care of its guests and the quality of food offered. AA and RAC***. Set in 25 acres of mature woodland with a private loch, it has excellent, comfortably appointed rooms, all with television, telephone, tea/coffee facilities and private bath or shower room. The elegant dining room enjoys a first class reputation for fine food and wine, with coffee afterwards in the comfortable drawing room. The grounds around the castle include a small loch with swans and ducks. Golf is available locally and St. Andrews is less than half an hour away by car.

[£] *Dinner, bed and breakfast £30 per person per night sharing twin room (minimum stay 3 nights).* 1st October to 31st March excluding Christmas, New Year and Public Holidays.

OLD MANOR HOTEL
Leven Road, Lundin Links KY8 6AJ
0333 320368 Fax: 0333 320911

A comfortable, friendly hotel, overlooking the famous Lundin Links golf course with views over the Forth to the Lothians. All bedrooms have private facilities, colour TV, radio, clock, direct-dial telephone, hairdryer, video films, tea/coffee facilities and complimentary newspaper. AA***, Egon Ronay and Michelin recommended. The restaurant specialises in fresh local produce, prepared to the highest standards. Cocktail bar with over 100 malts; Bunters Bar has live entertainment three nights a week. Wide range of sporting activities locally; ideal for exploring the fascinating Fife coastline. Weekend golf packages available.

[£] *Terms on request.*

Inverness-shire

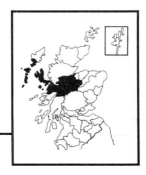

FAIRWINDS HOTEL
Carrbridge PH23 3AA
047-984 240

Highly Commended
♛ ♛ ♛ TA

AA Selected, RAC Acclaimed, STB ♛♛♛ Highly Commended. Fairwinds Hotel is set in mature pine woods some 200 yards back from the main road in the centre of the village, close to shops and local entertainment. Its five bedrooms all have private facilities, colour TV and tea/coffee making facilities. Our dining room offers a varied menu of good Scottish food; vegetarian meals and packed lunches by arrangement. The Hotel is licensed and drinks are available either in the lounge or with your meal. Sorry, no pets.

£ *From £54 per person for 2 nights dinner, bed and breakfast. Extra nights pro rata. Discount for children and Senior Citizens.* ⌕ *All year except Easter, July and August.*

LOCH NESS LODGE HOTEL
Drumnadrochit IV3 6TJ
04562 342

TA

Loch Ness Lodge Hotel dates from 1740 and is set in eight acres of varied woodland. Routiers Recommended. All bedrooms have private facilities, TV and a tea/coffee tray. On some evenings there is a very popular Scottish Country Show. Nearby is the Loch Ness Visitors' Centre, with a video show and gift shops. There are also cruises on the loch — with perhaps a glimpse of the famous monster!

£ *2 nights dinner, bed and breakfast from £50 per person.* ⌕ *October 1990 to April 1991.*

STAGE HOUSE INN
Glenfinnan PH37 4LT
039-783 246

Commended
♛ ♛ ♛

Personally run by the proprietors, the cosy and comfortable Stage House Inn offers attractively furnished guest rooms, with electric blankets, tea-makers and en suite facilities. Cuisine is of a high standard, using local produce and salmon, venison, shellfish and lobster when available. Extensive fishing rights on Loch Shiel are owned by the inn. This is an ideal base for exploring the beautiful Scottish Highlands — Fort William 15 miles, Kinlochleven 35 miles.

£ *3-day breaks dinner, bed and breakfast from £110.*

INVERMOY HOUSE PRIVATE HOTEL
Moy, Inverness IV13 7YE
08082 271

This unique hotel was originally a Highland Railway Station, now skilfully converted. Set amidst pinewoods and moorland. It lies eleven miles south of Inverness, and is centrally situated for touring the Highlands and Moray Firth area. Loch Ness is nearby, also the Cairngorms for ski-ing and other sports. All rooms are on the ground floor, and some of the seven bedrooms have private facilities. "Taste of Scotland". Table d'hôte dinner is served in the hotel dining room, or guests may dine à la carte in the Edwardian-style "Carriages Restaurant", converted from two railway coaches.

£ *For minimum 3 day stay dinner, bed and breakfast: from £23.75 per person per day (1 October to 31 March), from £26 per person per day 1 April to 30 September. Extra days pro rata.*

KILCOY CHALETS
Tore, By Muir of Ord, Near Inverness
0349 61456

TA

Chris and Ann's self-catering golfing package designed for golfing couples. Golf courses in the area include Royal Dornoch, Nairn, Fortrose, Muir of Ord, Strathpeffer and Inverness (all 18-hole). All year round breaks available in a high quality, well insulated, double glazed, cosy chalet designed for two. Only eight miles from Inverness, this peaceful, relaxing location is an ideal touring base for north and west Scotland.

£ *For 2 persons: from £275 per week; 3-day break £175. Reduction for single golfer. All year.*

EXPLANATION OF SYMBOLS

TA	Travel Agency Commission
♛	Number of Crowns
♀	Number of Keys
🐕	Pets Welcome
🐎	Reductions for Children
♿	Suitable for Disabled
🌲	Christmas Breaks

The symbols are arranged in the
same order throughout the book so that
looking down each page will give a quick comparison.

Inverness

Nairnshire

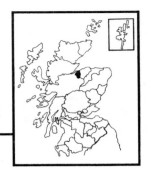

GOLF VIEW HOTEL
Nairn
0667 52301

Renowned for its excellent cuisine and service, the Golf View has something for everyone — heated outdoor pool, sauna, tennis, games and regular entertainment, plus the Nairn Championship Golf Course on the doorstep. All rooms have colour TV, telephone etc. Ideally situated for exploring this lovely part of Scotland — Inverness half an hour away, many fine golf courses in the area. Special Golf Packages available.

£ ***Details of Golf Packages and Weekend Specials available on request.***

Nairn from the River Nairn.

Perthshire

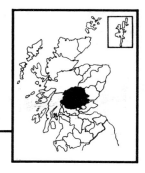

COLL EARN HOTEL
Auchterarder PH3 1DF
0764 63553 Fax: 0764 63059

Commended
♕ ♕ ♕

Situated in the heart of the beautiful Perthshire countryside, this delightful hotel is a marvellous tribute to the extravagance and eccentricities of Victorian architecture, with beautiful wood panelling and fascinating stained glass. Bedrooms are spacious and luxurious and all have private facilities. In the intimate dining room the constantly changing menu offers the finest traditional Scottish and European cuisine, all beautifully prepared. Set in its own grounds yet easily accessible from the M90 Edinburgh/Perth motorway, this is an ideal place to find true peace and quiet.

£ **£43-£57 per day for dinner, bed and breakfast, based on stays of 3 days or more.** ☐ **All year.**

BRIDGE OF CALLY HOTEL
By Blairgowrie PH10 7JJ
025086 231

♕ ♕ ♕
🐕 🐎

The hotel is situated six miles north of Blairgowrie in the beautiful Perthshire countryside. Nine bedrooms, six with private facilities. Comfortable residents' lounge with colour TV, warm and friendly cocktail bar. AA*, RAC**, Egon Ronay and Ashley Courtenay recommended. The area abounds in walks; pony trekking is available. Golf at Rosemount with other fine courses around. Ideally situated for Braemar, Glamis and Pitlochry. Perth 20 miles.

£ **£60 dinner, bed and breakfast per person for 2 day break.** ☐ **All year except August, September, November, Christmas and New Year.**

ARDEN HOUSE
Bracklinn Road, Callander FK17 8EQ
0877 30235

Commended
♕ ♕ ♕ [TA]
🐕 🐎

Set peacefully in its own attractive gardens and enjoying outstanding views over the Perthshire countryside, Arden House has a warm and friendly atmosphere in which to enjoy a relaxing holiday. All bedrooms have central heating, washbasins, shaver points, electric blankets and teamakers. Most rooms en suite. Putting green and children's play area. Arden House is ideally situated for touring beautiful Perthshire, and it was the TV home of *Dr Finlay's Casebook*.

£ **Dinner, bed and breakfast from £20. Minimum 2 nights stay.** ☐ **October, November, February, March and April.**

Perthshire 139

NEWTON HOUSE HOTEL
Glencarse, By Perth PH2 7LX
073-886 250

This RAC/AA*** Hotel was a former Dower House and is situated only 4 miles from Perth and 13 from Dundee. It is an ideal base to explore the dramatic countryside and numerous places of interest such as Glamis Castle, Scone Palace and world famous golf courses. All en suite rooms overlook the gardens and daily change dinner menus utilise fresh local produce. Our recipes are featured in the prestigious "Taste of Scotland Guide".

£ *Your hosts Geoffrey and Carol Tallis offer 2 days dinner, bed and breakfast from £88. Please ask for our brochure.* All year.

KILLIECRANKIE HOTEL
Pass of Killiecrankie, By Pitlochry PH16 5LG
0796 3220

Delightful converted dower house in four acres of grounds, overlooking the famous Pass of Killiecrankie and RSPB Bird Reserve. All bedrooms tastefully and individually decorated, most en suite. There is a fully licensed cocktail bar and comfortable residents' lounge. The hotel is justifiably renowned for its food. Lunches and suppers served in the bar. BTA Commended. Good Food Guide. Pitlochry has one of Scotland's premier theatres and the area offers scope for anglers, golfers and walkers.

£ *From £96.50 per person for 2 nights bed, breakfast and excellent dinner (inc. VAT). Longer breaks also available.* From February 1991.

LION AND UNICORN
Thornhill, By Stirling FK8 3PJ
078-685 204

Some say Perthshire is at its most beautiful in the autumn, and a cosy base from which to discover its out-of-season charms is provided in this 300-year-old inn, where a log-burning stove adds cheer as well as additional warmth to the convivial lounge. Bedrooms are well appointed and comfortable, and wholesome meals and snacks can be enjoyed in the bar and restaurant. Darts and dominoes are played in the public bar and the inn has its own bowling green. Good Pub Guide.

£ *3 nights half board £49 per person.* September to April.

HOLIDAY ACCOMMODATION
Classification Schemes in England, Scotland and Wales

The National Tourist Boards for England, Scotland and Wales have agreed a common 'Crown Classification' scheme for **serviced (Board)** accommodation. All establishments are inspected regularly and are given a classification indicating their level of facilities and services.

There are six grades ranging from 'Listed' to 'Five Crowns ♛♛♛♛♛'. The higher the classification, the more facilities and services offered. Crown classification is a measure of *facilities* not *quality*. A common quality grading scheme grades the quality of establishments as 'Approved', 'Commended' or 'Highly Commended' according to the accommodation, welcome and service they provide.

For **Self-Catering**, holiday homes in England are awarded 'Keys' after inspection and can also be 'Approved', 'Commended' or 'Highly Commended' according to the facilities available. In Scotland the Crown scheme includes self-catering accommodation and Wales also has a voluntary inspection scheme for self-catering grading from '1 (Standard)' to '5 (Excellent)'.

Caravan and Camping Parks can participate in the British Holiday Parks grading scheme from 'Approved (√)' to 'Excellent (√ √ √ √ √)'. In addition, each National Tourist Board has an annual award for high-quality caravan accommodation: in England – Rose Awards; in Scotland – Thistle Commendations; in Wales – Dragon Awards.

When advertisers supply us with the information, FHG Publications show Crowns and other awards or gradings, including AA, RAC, Egon Ronay etc. We also award a small number of Farm Holiday Guide Diplomas every year, based on readers' recommendations.

Ross-shire

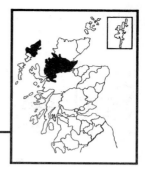

CRAIGDARROCH LODGE HOTEL
Contin-by-Strathpeffer IV14 9EH
0997 21265

[TA]

Golfing, sailing, fishing, shooting, touring, walking — or simply just relaxing — let us tailor a short break holiday to your requirements. Idyllically situated in 8 acres of garden and woodland, beautiful walking country, secluded and peaceful, central for touring, Craigdarroch is ideal for your Highland short break holiday. Indoor facilities include swimming pool, sauna, solarium and snooker; outdoors there is tennis, fishing and croquet. Whenever you visit you can be sure of superb cuisine, attentive service and a friendly, relaxed atmosphere, all combining to make this a holiday to remember. AA/RAC**, Egon Ronay.

[£] *From £75 per person for 3 nights dinner, bed and breakfast.*

ROYAL HOTEL
Fortrose IV10 8SU
0381 20236

Commended

Treat yourself to a relaxing break in our small, family-run hotel in the conservation village of Fortrose, 20 minutes' drive from Inverness. Excellent 18-hole golf course and three-quarters of an hour's drive from the championship course at Dornoch. Ideal location for touring the Highlands. The well-appointed bedrooms have electric blankets and tea/coffee making facilities; many are en suite. The Royal has a comfortable residents' lounge, two bars and a dining room serving bar snacks and meals daily, using the best of local produce.

[£] *Dinner, bed and full Scottish breakfast £24 per person per night inc. VAT. En suite room. Minimum 2 nights.* Mid-January to first week in December.

PUBLISHER'S NOTE

While every effort is made to ensure accuracy, we regret that FHG Publications cannot accept responsibility for errors, omissions or misrepresentation in our entries or any consequences thereof. Prices in particular should be checked because we go to press early. We will follow up complaints but cannot act as arbiters or agents for either party.

Stirlingshire

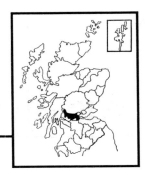

COVENANTERS INN
Aberfoyle FK8 3XD
08772 347 Telex: 778481

Nestling in the foothills of the world-famous Trossachs, the Covenanters Inn is set in woodlands overlooking the River Forth and the village of Aberfoyle. Renowned for its olde worlde charm and hospitality, and with log fires, oak beams and cosy small lounges, the Covenanters Inn provides a relaxed comfortable ambience. Coupled with the warm welcome which awaits you, the traditional Scottish menus in the restaurant will make your visit pleasant and memorable. All rooms have private facilities, colour TV etc.

£ *2 nights dinner, bed and breakfast from £30 per person per night.* October to April.

THE ROYAL HOTEL
55 Henderson Street, Bridge of Allan FK9 4HG
0786 832284

This impressive Victorian hotel has been carefully restored and refurbished throughout to produce an atmosphere of splendour and elegance. All bedrooms are en suite, with radio and television, direct-dial telephones and tea/coffee making facilities. The restaurant is noted for its fine selection of fresh Scottish produce prepared in the classic French style. Guests can relax in the oak-panelled lounge or in the friendly "Kings" bar. Stirling is rich in historical associations, and provides a wide range of shopping, sports and leisure facilities. AA and RAC***, Egon Ronay, Ashley Courtenay.

£ *£35 per person per night, dinner, bed and breakfast. Minimum 2 nights Fri./Sat./Sun.* 1st October-30th April.

EXPLANATION OF SYMBOLS

TA	Travel Agency Commission
♛	Number of Crowns
⚷	Number of Keys
🐕	Pets Welcome
🐎	Reductions for Children
♿	Suitable for Disabled
🎄	Christmas Breaks

142 *Stirlingshire*

Wigtownshire

STEAM PACKET INN
Harbour Row, Isle of Whithorn DG8 8LL
098-85 334

This attractive little quayside hotel, run by John Scoular and his wife, has a reputation which stretches far beyond the picturesque little town it graces. Overnight accommodation is available in five delightfully furnished guest rooms, all with beverage making facilities, colour television and private bathroom. Michelin Good Pub Guide. Food is well prepared, plentiful and also moderately priced, and can be served in the beamed dining room or in the bar which looks out to the harbour. Residents have free access to golf on the local course.

£ *Terms on application.*

Orkney

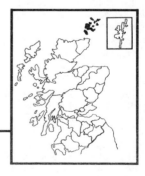

STROMNESS HOTEL
Stromness
0856 850298

Comfortable 42-bedroomed hotel situated in the heart of the unique fishing port of Stromness, which is also the main ferry terminal between the mainland and the Orkneys. The hotel overlooks the harbour and Scapa Flow, which served as the British naval base for the last two World Wars. All bedrooms have en suite bathrooms, colour TV and tea-making facilities. The hotel offers a large lounge bar with regular entertainment, public bar, dining room. There is also a restaurant which comes highly recommended.

£ *Terms on application.*

ONE FOR YOUR FRIEND 1991

FHG Publications have a large range of attractive holiday accommodation guides for all kinds of holiday opportunities throughout Britain. They also make useful gifts at any time of year. Our guides are available in most bookshops and larger newsagents but we will be happy to post you a copy direct if you have any difficulty. We will also post abroad but have to charge separately for post or freight.

The inclusive cost of posting and packing the guides to you or your friends in the UK is as follows:

Farm Holiday Guide ENGLAND, WALES and IRELAND
Board, Self-catering, Caravans/Camping, Activity Holidays. About 600 pages. **£3.60**

Farm Holiday Guide SCOTLAND
All kinds of holiday accommodation. **£2.60**

SELF-CATERING & FURNISHED HOLIDAYS
Over 1000 addresses throughout for Self-catering and caravans in Britain. **£3.00**

BRITAIN'S BEST HOLIDAYS
A quick-reference general guide for all kinds of holidays. **£2.50**

The FHG Guide to CARAVAN & CAMPING HOLIDAYS
Caravans for hire, sites and holiday parks and centres. **£2.60**

BED AND BREAKFAST STOPS
Over 1000 friendly and comfortable overnight stops. **£3.00**

CHILDREN WELCOME! FAMILY HOLIDAY GUIDE
Family holidays with details of amenities for children and babies. **£2.50**

Recommended SHORT BREAK HOLIDAYS IN BRITAIN
'Approved' accommodation for quality bargain breaks. Introduced by John Carter. **£3.50**

Recommended COUNTRY HOTELS OF BRITAIN
Including Country Houses, for the discriminating. **£3.50**

Recommended WAYSIDE INNS OF BRITAIN
Pubs, Inns and small hotels. **£3.50**

PGA GOLF GUIDE Where to play and where to stay
Over 2000 golf courses with convenient accommodation. Endorsed by the PGA. **£6.50**

PETS WELCOME!
The unique guide for holidays for pet owners and their pets. **£3.00**

BED AND BREAKFAST IN BRITAIN
Over 1000 choices for touring and holidays throughout Britain. **£2.50**

LONDON'S BEST BED AND BREAKFAST HOTELS
Inspected and recommended with prices. Over 120 safe, clean and friendly small hotels. **£3.25**

THE FRENCH FARM AND VILLAGE HOLIDAY GUIDE
The official guide to self-catering holidays in the 'Gîtes de France'. **£7.50**

Tick your choice and send your order and payment to FHG PUBLICATIONS, ABBEY MILL BUSINESS CENTRE, SEEDHILL, PAISLEY PA1 1JN (TEL: 041-887 0428. FAX: 041-889 7204). **Deduct** 10% for 2/3 titles or copies; 20% for 4 or more.

Send to: NAME ....

ADDRESS ....

....

.... POST CODE ....

I enclose Cheque/Postal Order for £ ....

SIGNATURE .... DATE ....

MAP SECTION

The following seven pages of maps indicate the main cities, towns and holiday centres of Britain. Space obviously does not permit every location featured in this book to be included but the approximate position may be ascertained by using the distance indications quoted and the scale bars on the maps.

Map 1

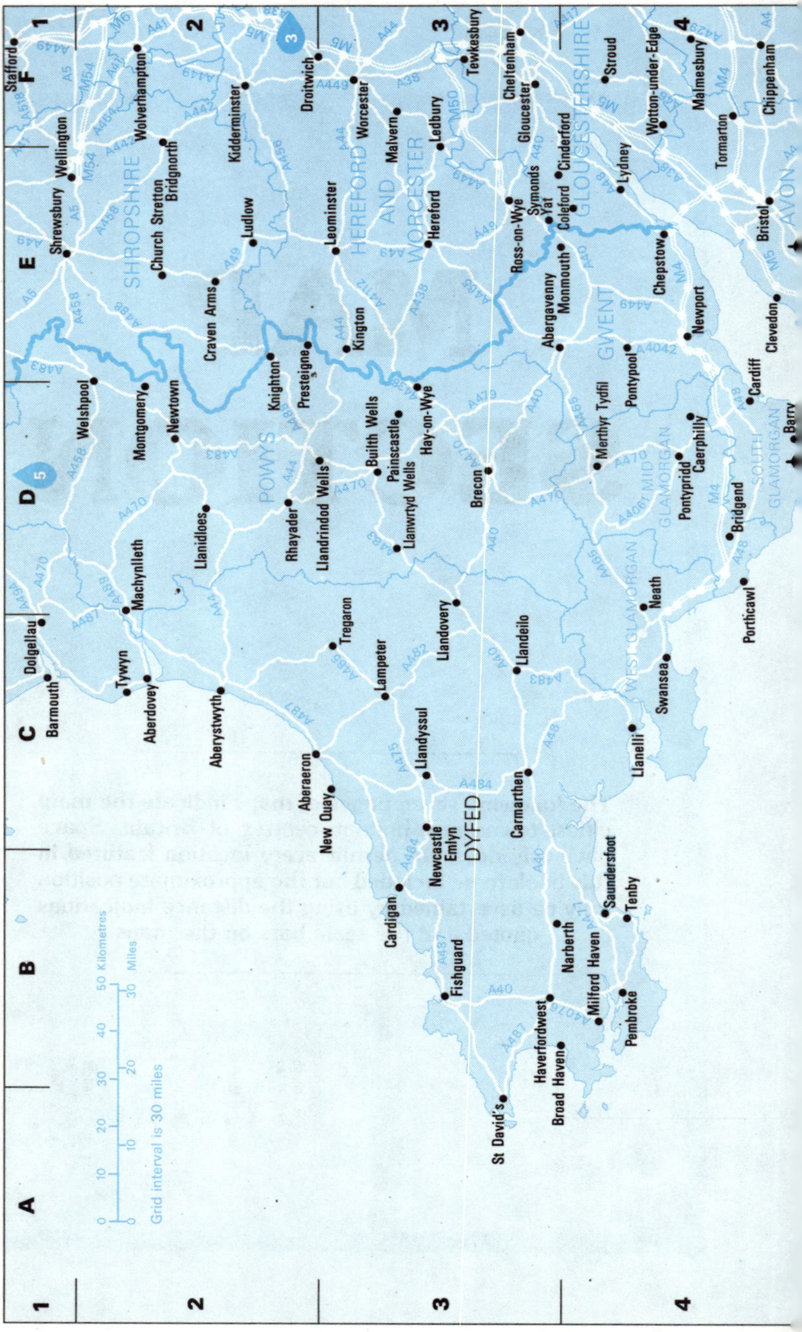
A
B
C
D
E
F
1
2
3
4
Stafford
Wellington
Wolverhampton
Shrewsbury
Church Stretton
Bridgnorth
Kidderminster
Droitwich
Worcester
Malvern
Ledbury
Tewkesbury
Cheltenham
Gloucester
Ludlow
Leominster
Hereford
Ross-on-Wye
Symonds Yat
Coleford
Cinderford
Stroud
Lydney
Wotton-under-Edge
Malmesbury
Tormarton
Chippenham
Bristol
Clevedon
Chepstow
Newport
Monmouth
Abergavenny
Pontypool
Cardiff
Barry
Caerphilly
Pontypridd
Merthyr Tydfil
Bridgend
Porthcawl
Neath
Swansea
Llanelli
Kington
Presteigne
Knighton
Craven Arms
Welshpool
Montgomery
Newtown
Llanidloes
Rhayader
Llandrindod Wells
Builth Wells
Painscastle
Hay-on-Wye
Llanwrtyd Wells
Brecon
Llandovery
Llandeilo
Tregaron
Lampeter
Machynlleth
Dolgellau
Barmouth
Tywyn
Aberdovey
Aberystwyth
Aberaeron
New Quay
Llandyssul
Newcastle Emlyn
Cardigan
Carmarthen
Fishguard
Narberth
Saundersfoot
Tenby
Haverfordwest
Milford Haven
Pembroke
Broad Haven
St David's
SHROPSHIRE
HEREFORD AND WORCESTER
GLOUCESTERSHIRE
AVON
GWENT
POWYS
DYFED
MID GLAMORGAN
SOUTH GLAMORGAN
WEST GLAMORGAN
0 10 20 30 40 50 Kilometres
0 10 20 30 Miles
Grid interval is 30 miles

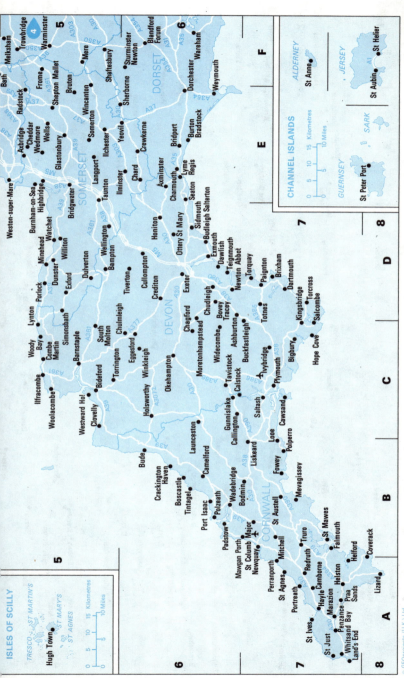

Map 3

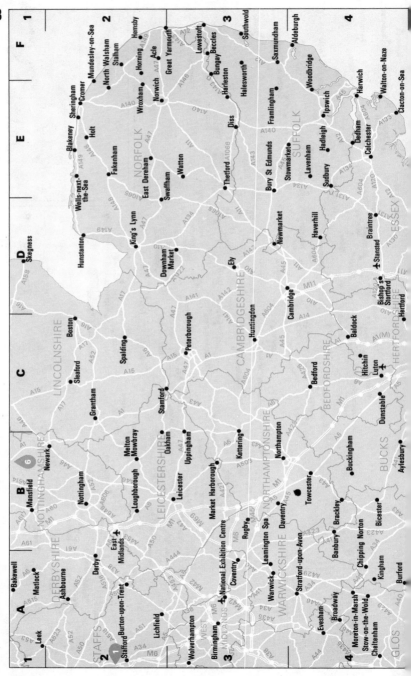

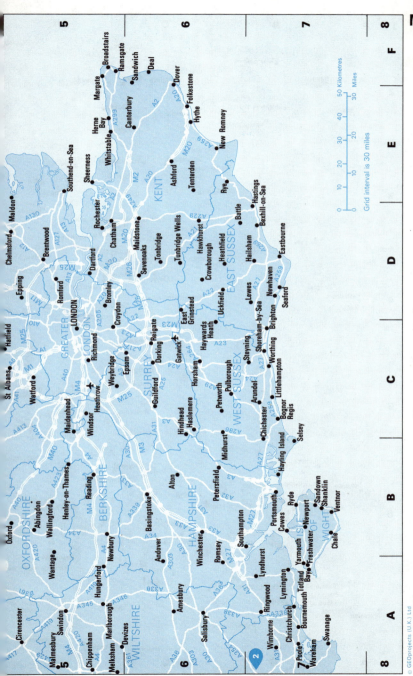

Map 4

Map 5

Map 6

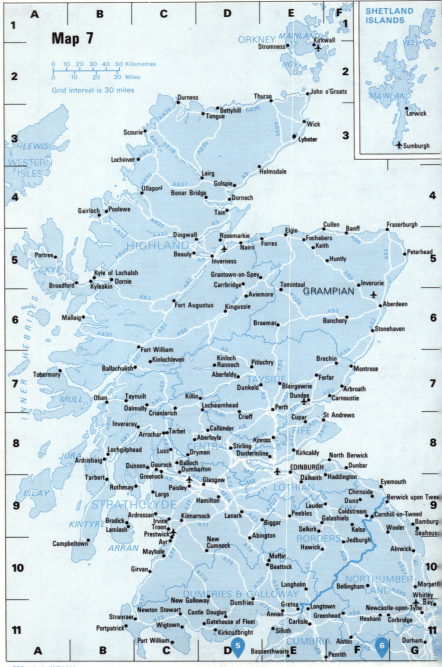